This is a story about a dog called Garm, a cow called Galathea, who comes to a sticky end, a deaf and rather short-sighted giant, whose name we never hear, and a farmer called Giles, who doesn't like trespassers.

The story is taken from *Farmer Giles of Ham*, by J. R. R. Tolkien.

Giant!

It was a fine night. The cows were in the fields, and Farmer Giles's dog had got out and gone for a walk on his own account. He had a fancy for moonshine, and rabbits. He had no idea, of course, that a giant was also out for a walk. That would have given him a good reason for going out without leave, but a still better reason for staying quiet in the kitchen. At about two o'clock the giant arrived in Farmer Giles's fields, broke the hedges, trampled on the crops, and flattened the mowing-grass. In five minutes he had done more damage than the royal fox-hunt could have done in five days.

Garm heard a thump-thump coming along the river-bank, and he ran to the west side of the low hill on which the farmhouse stood, just to see what was happening. Suddenly he saw the giant stride right across the river and tread upon Galathea, the farmer's favourite cow, squashing the poor beast as flat as the farmer could have squashed a blackbeetle.

That was more than enough for Garm. He gave a yelp of fright and bolted home. Quite forgetting that he was out without leave, he came and barked and yammered underneath his master's bedroom window. There was no answer for a long time. Farmer Giles was not easily wakened.

'Help! help! help!' cried Garm.

The window opened suddenly and a well-aimed bottle came flying out.

'Ow!' said the dog, jumping aside with practised skill. 'Help! help! help!'

Out popped the farmer's head. 'Drat you, dog! What be you a-doing?' said he.

'Nothing,' said the dog.

2

'I'll give you nothing! I'll flay the skin off you in the morning,' said the farmer, slamming the window.

'Help! help! help!' cried the dog.

Out came Giles's head again. 'I'll kill you, if you make another sound,' he said. 'What's come to you, you fool?'

'Nothing,' said the dog; 'but something's come to you.'

'What d'you mean?' said Giles, startled in the midst of his rage. Never before had Garm answered him saucily.

'There's a giant in your fields, an enormous giant; and he's coming this way,' said the dog. 'Help! help! He is trampling on your sheep. He has stamped on poor Galathea, and she's as flat as a doormat. Help! help! He's bursting all your hedges, and he's crushing all your crops. You must be bold and quick, master, or you will soon have nothing left. Help!' Garm began to howl.

'Shut up!' said the farmer, and he shut the window. 'Lord-a-mercy!' he said to himself; and though the night was warm, he shivered and shook.

'Get back to bed and don't be a fool!' said his wife. 'And drown that dog in the morning. There is no call to believe what a dog says: they'll tell any tale, when caught truant or thieving.'

'May be, Agatha,' said he, 'and may be not. But there's something going on in my fields, or Garm's a rabbit. That dog was frightened. And why should he come yammering in the night when he could sneak in at the back door with the milk in the morning?'

'Don't stand there arguing!' said she. 'If you believe the dog, then take his advice: be bold and quick!'

'Easier said than done,' answered Giles; for, indeed, he believed quite half of Garm's tale. In the small hours of the night giants seem less unlikely.

Still, property is property; and Farmer Giles had a short way with trespassers that few could outface. So he pulled on his breeches, and went down into the kitchen and took his blunderbuss from the wall ... and he put in a good charge of powder, just in case extreme measures should be required; and into the wide mouth he stuffed old nails and bits of wire, pieces of broken pot, bones and stones and other rubbish. Then he drew on his top-boots and his overcoat, and he went out through the kitchen garden.

3

The moon was low behind him, and he could see nothing worse than the long black shadows of bushes and trees; but he could hear a dreadful stamping-stumping coming up the side of the hill. He did not feel either bold or quick, whatever Agatha might say; but he was more anxious about his property than his skin. So, feeling a bit loose about the belt, he walked towards the brow of the hill.

Suddenly up over the edge of it the giant's face appeared, pale in the moonlight, which glittered in his large round eyes. His feet were still far below, making holes in the fields. The moon dazzled the giant and he did not see the farmer; but Farmer Giles saw him and was scared out of his wits. He pulled the trigger without thinking, and the blunderbuss went off with a staggering bang. By luck it was pointed more or less at the giant's large ugly face.

Out flew the rubbish, and the stones and the bones, and the bits of crock and wire, and half a dozen nails. And since the range was indeed limited, by chance and no choice of the farmer's many of these things struck the giant: a piece of pot went in his eye, and a large nail stuck in his nose.

'Blast!' said the giant in his vulgar fashion. 'I'm stung!' The noise had made no impression on him (he was rather deaf), but he did not like the nail. It was a long time since he had met any insect fierce enough to pierce his thick skin; but he had heard tell

that away East, in the Fens, there were dragonflies that could bite like hot pincers. He thought that he must have run into something of the kind.

'Nasty unhealthy parts, evidently,' said he. 'I shan't go any further this way tonight.'

So he picked up a couple of sheep off the hill-side, to eat when he got home, and went back over the river, making off about nor-nor-west at a great pace. He found his way home again in the end, for he was at last going in the right direction; but the bottom was burned off his copper pot.

As for Farmer Giles, when the blunderbuss went off it knocked him over flat on his back; and there he lay looking at the sky and wondering if the giant's feet would miss him as they passed by. But nothing happened, and the stamping-stumping died away in the distance. So he got up, rubbed his shoulder, and picked up the blunderbuss. Then suddenly he heard the sound of people cheering.

Most of the people of Ham had been looking out of their windows; a few had put on their clothes and come out (after the giant had gone away). Some were now running up the hill shouting.

The villagers had heard the horrible thump-thump of the giant's feet, and most of them had immediately got under the bed-clothes; some had got under the beds. But Garm was both proud and frightened of his master. He thought him terrible and splendid, when he was angry; and he naturally thought that any giant would think the same. So, as soon as he saw Giles come out with the blunderbuss (a sign of great wrath as a rule), he rushed off to the village, barking and crying:

'Come out! Come out! Come out! Get up! Get up! Come and see my great master! He is bold and quick. He is going to shoot a giant for trespassing. Come out!'

The top of the hill could be seen from most of the houses. When the people and the dog saw the giant's face rise above it, they quailed and held their breath, and all but the dog among them thought that this would prove a matter too big for Giles to deal with. Then the blunderbuss went bang, and the giant turned suddenly and went away, and in their amazement and their joy they clapped and cheered, and Garm nearly barked his head off.

'Hooray!' they shouted. 'That will learn him! Master Aegidius has given him what for. Now he will go home and die, and serve him right and proper.' Then they all cheered again together. But even as they cheered, they took note for their own profit that after all this blunderbuss could really be fired. There had been some debate in the village inns on that point; but now the matter was settled. Farmer Giles had little trouble with trespassers after that.

To think and talk about

A 1. The dog does not normally get out alone at night. How do we know? What would usually happen to him if he went out alone at night? Why did he go out?

2. Can you find any clues in the story to tell how big the Giant is?

3. Does Giles really think the dog is a liar? How do you know? Does Agatha think the dog is a liar? Why do you think so?

4. What did Giles expect to find in his fields? Did he go out intending to fire the blunderbuss? Why was the firing of the blunderbuss so important to the villagers, apart from the fact that it got rid of the giant?

5. How much can you tell about the giant from the story? How intelligent is he? How do you know?

6. Is the dog really afraid of Giles? What does he think of his master? How many clues to this can you find in the story?

B 1. Do you think the people like the royal fox hunt? Why do you think so?

2. The story gives the idea that Garm is a coward. Is this really true, or can you find clues to say that he is brave?

3. 'In the small hours of the night, giants seemed less unlikely.' What does this sentence mean? Do you agree with it? Why?

4. What do you think the villagers thought of Giles before the giant came?
Do you think their opinion of him changed after he frightened away the giant?
In what ways?

5. Do you think Agatha always does as her husband tells her? Who do you think really rules their house? Why do you say so?

6. How would you have felt about going out to face a giant, if you had been Farmer Giles? Would your feelings have been different afterwards? In what ways?

9

More books to read

1. *Smith of Wootton Major* by J. R. R. Tolkein
   What is the star in the cake at the feast in the village of Wootton Major? You *must* read this enthralling story, and don't forget this writer's famous book *The Hobbit*.

2. *Collected Stories for Children* by Walter de la Mare
   You will enjoy the stories in this book. Some long, some short, all exciting.

3. *The Battle of Bubble and Squeak* by Philippa Pearce
   Sid and Peggy love their two gerbils Bubble and Squeak. Trouble is their mother detests them. You'll enjoy reading how the family battle progresses.

Spot the howler

For sale, antique shotgun, one owner with new firing mechanism.

Can you say what is odd about this sentence?

At the local football club the manager keeps a shop and coaches.

Ideas to write about

1. Imagine you are Garm, talking to a friend.
Tell the story of how you met the Giant, and what your
master, Giles, did after he had taken his blunderbuss from the
wall.

2. The Giant was a shock for Giles, when he arrived that night in
the fields.
Imagine that you are sitting quietly in school one day,
working as usual, when you hear the thump, thump of giant
footsteps, and you look up to see an enormous giant striding
down the road towards your school.
Write the story of what happens.

Word pairs

Below are two sets of words. Each word in set A has a partner in
set B which sounds exactly the same, although it is spelt
differently. Can you write down the partners?

Set A	Set B
flea	maid
find	grown
groan	flee
made	male
mail	fowl
foul	fined

Carol has found a poem about a giant.

Giant Thunder

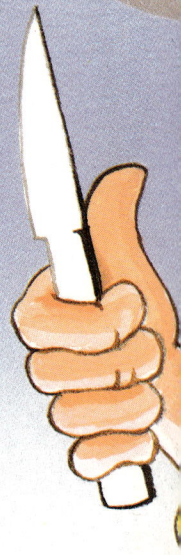

Giant Thunder, striding home,
Wonders if his supper's done.

'Hag wife, hag wife, bring me my bones!'
'They are not done,' the old hag moans.

'Not done? Not done?' the giant roars
And heaves his old wife out of doors.

Cries he, 'I'll have them, cooked or not!'
But overturns the cooking-pot.

He flings the burning coals about;
See how the lightning flashes out.

Upon the gale the old hag rides,
The cloudy moon for terror hides.

All the world with thunder quakes;
Forest shudders, mountain shakes;
From the cloud the rainstorm breaks;
Village ponds are turned to lakes;
Every living creature wakes.

Hungry Giant, lie you still!
Stamp no more from hill to hill —
Tomorrow you shall have your fill.

James Reeves

Searching for missing words

In the story below some words have been missed out.
Can you be sure which words have been missed out?
Sometimes there can be only one answer.
Sometimes there can be several answers for you to think and talk about.
How many words can you find?

The children crouched behind its spread tail, almost afraid to draw their breath, until the sentry shouldered his halberd and continued his patrol. Then, as the _____ went behind another cloud, darkness swept the garden _____ a black flood. They seized their chance and _____ silently for the arched gate in the wall.

_____ they gained the safety of the park, the moon _____ out once more. But it hung low in _____ sky now, touching the treetops beyond the lake. _____ the ragged clouds streamed across the silver _____. When they had passed, the moon had sunk _____ the wooded ridge. Nick knew it would be _____ than ever now for the next hour, until _____ day began to break.

Still, they could just _____ where they were going, and it was all _____ ground. Long, low bands of mist rose from the _____ in front, glimmering and ghostly pale against the _____ of the night.

From *A Masque for the Queen* by Geoffrey Trease

How to use a book

Going to the Library

Have you ever been to a public library? If not, you should!
They are very interesting places.
Most libraries have four sections (at least):

1. **children's library**
2. **fiction**
3. **non-fiction**
4. **reference**

Can you think what sections 2, 3 and 4 contain?
Have you any idea of the difference between sections 3 and 4?

Here is a tiny part of a fiction list in a library.

> Abbott, James: *Tales of Mystery*
> Acker, Jane: *The Stroke of Twelve*
> Booth, Coraline: *No Smoke Without Fire*
> Burton, Steve: *Blazing Guns*
> Butters, Yvonne: *Three Can Play*
> Cather, Ella: *Night Must End*

The books here are put on the shelves according to the author's name.
Is this the way it is done in
   your school library?
   your public library?

Can you find out how the **non-fiction** books are arranged in both these libraries?
There can be more than one way.
Which way do *you* think may be the easiest, to help you find a book?

Funny words

What word do you think the artist has made a drawing of in this picture?

There are lots of words which are funny if you think about them. Talk about how you might make a funny drawing of the word

childhood

Can you draw a picture for **childhood**?

What are they saying?

Look at what is happening in this picture. What do you think they might be saying?

My dad's thumb

My dad's thumb
can stick pins in wood
without flinching —
it can crush family-size matchboxes
in one stroke
and lever off jam-jar lids without piercing
at the pierce here sign.

If it wanted
it could be a bath-plug
or a paint-scraper
a keyhole cover or a tap-tightener.

It's already a great nutcracker
and if it dressed up
it could easily pass
as a broad bean or a big toe.

In actual fact, it's quite simply
the world's fastest envelope burster.

Michael Rosen

Check your facts

The Owl and the Mouse

The owl sat in its cage without moving. Its eyes were fixed on the ground where a small field mouse was quietly munching a piece of turnip. Forgetting for a moment that it was enclosed by bars the owl launched itself silently off its perch. Its journey came to a noisy and sudden end when it hit the bars and fell to the bottom of the cage. For a second it remained there. With a sad and angry look it glanced to where the mouse was still quietly eating. The field mouse was unaware that it could easily have provided a small snack for a large owl.

Here are some sentences about the passage.
Put them into three groups:
- (a) True
- (b) Untrue
- (c) Nothing to do with the passage

1. Plants need water to grow.

2. A broken wing stopped the owl from catching the mouse.

3. When the owl fell down it was not happy.

4. The owl was planning to eat the mouse.

5. The owl was trying to escape from its cage.

6. A wishing well should be built in every city.

7. The owl tried a second time to catch the mouse.

8. Birds eat worms.

9. The mouse was having its dinner.

10. The owl forgot it was in a cage.

11. All animals like to be chased.

12. The mouse was frightened by the owl.

Ideas to write about

Ruth made up an imaginary interview with Farmer Giles, so she could write about him for the school newspaper. Here is some of what she imagined them saying to each other.

Ruth: What first woke you up, Farmer Giles?

Giles: Well, it was my dog, Garm, shouting at the window. I was fast asleep, but he woke me up.

Ruth: What time was this?

Giles:

Ruth: Why did he wake you?

Giles:

Ruth: Did you believe him?

Giles:

Ruth: What did you do?

Giles:

What do you think Farmer Giles's missing answers might be? Can you think of some more questions to ask?

Crossword

Can you make up clues for this crossword?

¹h	o	²r	s	³e
e	■	o	■	a
a	■	s	■	s
r	■	e	■	e
⁴t	a	s	k	s

Across

1.

4.

Down

1.

2.

3.

Reading for the main idea

Survival

Three weeks after they were born the five young rabbits ventured above ground for the first time. At first they stayed close to their mother but soon they began to explore further afield, nibbling the fresh green shoots of grass and clover. Suddenly a warning signal was given—the stamping of hind feet on the ground. There was a quick dash back to the burrow but alas one youngster was not quick enough to heed the danger sign and was caught in the talons of a swooping hawk. His piercing death cries were the first hard lesson that his brothers and sisters were to learn.

Thomas made notes of the main ideas in the story. Here is what he wrote:

— **five rabbits go out for the first time**
— **wandered away from mother**.

Think of the other main ideas in the story.
Add them to Thomas's list so that you have notes on all the main ideas.
Talk about the notes you made.
Does everyone agree about the main ideas?

Ideas to write about

This picture is part of a story.
Write the story which you think it is part of.

The company words keep

Davina's class was asked to think of as many words as possible which might be used if writing or talking about the idea of **darkness**.

Here are some of the answers they gave:

gloomy	**black**	**creepy**	**eerie**
pitch	**murky**	**evil**	**frightening**

Can you see why these words have something to do with **darkness**?

Talk about the words. How many more can you think of which fit the idea of **darkness**?

Next, Davina's class was asked to suggest *ideas* which they thought went with darkness.

Here are some of the ideas they thought of.

Davina: Trees seeming to come to life in the dark.
Cheryl: Unknown things lurking round corners.
Nasim: Being lost in a tunnel and very scared.
Alan: Sitting with closed eyes listening to music.

Can you see why these ideas might go with darkness?
How many more ideas like these can you think of?

With your friends, talk about the words which you might use if you were talking or writing about the idea of **light**.
How many can you think of?
What ideas can you think of which are **light** ideas?

Act it out

Carrie's group was asked to act the scene from the story 'Giant!'
when Garm returned to the farm with news of the giant.

First they talked about the voices of the three characters, Garm,
Farmer Giles, and Agatha.
How do you think Garm the dog would speak? Are there clues in
the story to tell you?
What about Giles and Agatha?

Next the children looked at what was said by the characters.
They talked about the expressions which would be on the faces
of the characters.
How would Giles's face look at the beginning?
What about Garm?
Would their faces change during the scene?
What about Agatha's face?

Can you decide on the way the words should be said?
Try to give your face the right expression.

Why not try acting the scene?

Giving instructions

This is a plan of part of the town where Billy lives.
Billy wrote down a list of instructions for Lorna to get to his house on Saturday. Here it is:

1. Turn right at garden gate.

2. Go along Cedar Place and turn right into Elm Lane.

3. Cross Elm Lane at crossing, to turn left into Main Road.

4. Cross Main Road at zebra crossing.

5. Turn left at end of crossing.

6. My house is through the first gate you come to after the zebra crossing.

Zebra Crossing

Elm St

Elm Lane

Billy's House

Main Road

Corner shop

Water La

Can you write instructions to guide Lorna home from school?
Start like this:

1. Go out of school gate and turn left.

There are several ways she could go.

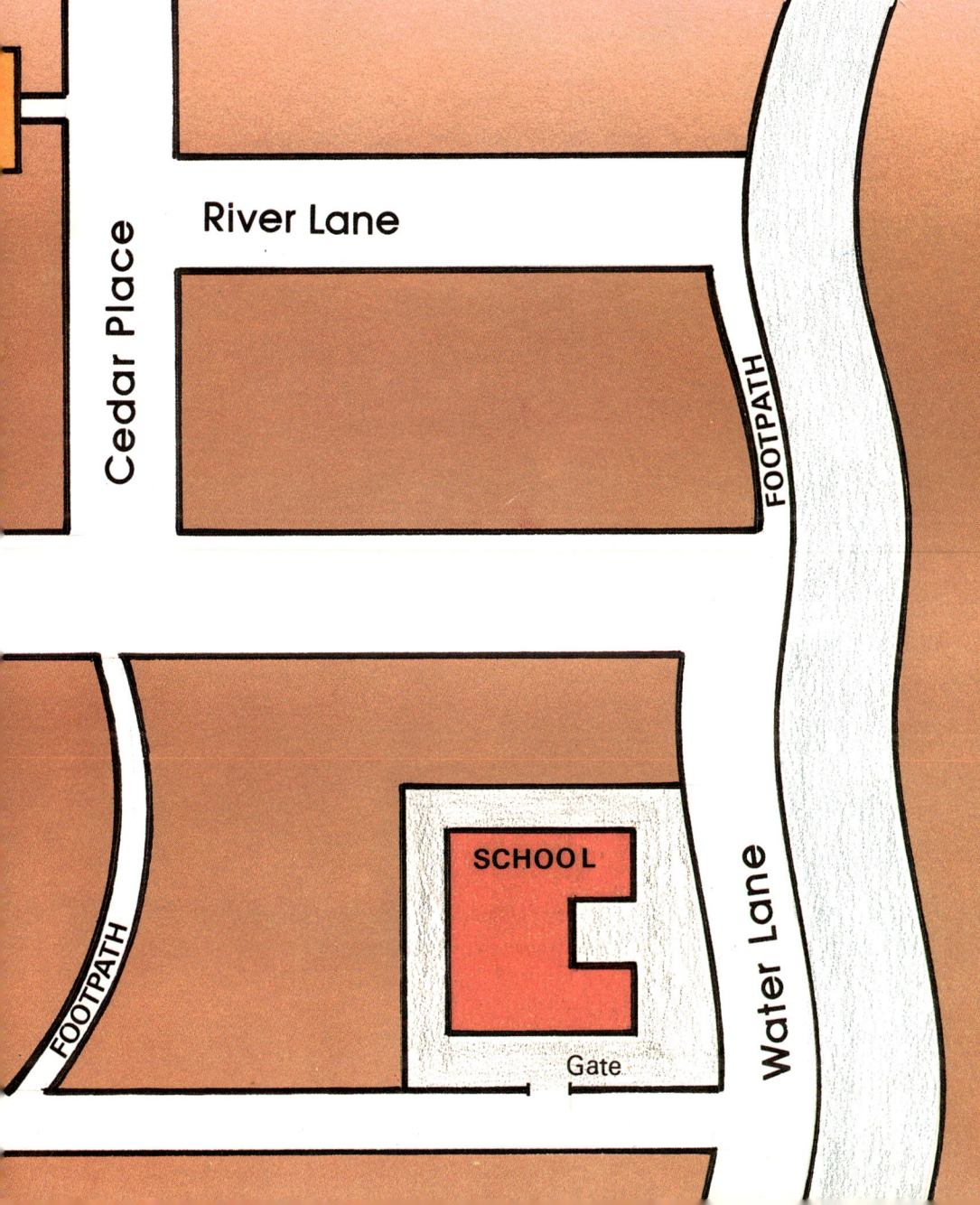

The way words are built

Sometimes to make a word simpler to say, or to make it take up less space, we make it shorter.
You can often see shortened words in newspapers.
Below are some headlines which you might see in a newspaper.
Each shortened word is underlined. Can you say exactly what each means?

CHOC BAR KIDS

'CIGS KILL' TAG IS RULED OUT

Sock it to em, Grandma

A merry Xmas!

Cannonball Cowans blasts the Aussies

Co-op official

WORLD of TELLY

HELI HORROR

Look at a newspaper. Can you find more shortened words like these?

Can you tell which shortened word we get from the following?

omnibus	veterinary surgeon
television	bicycle
aeroplane	telephone

Talk about how the words have become shortened.
Can you find any more words which you think have been shortened?

26

Ted Hughes wrote a book of stories about how God made various animals, including the Whale, the Elephant, the Donkey and the Bee.

This story comes from *How the Whale Became, and Other Stories* by Ted Hughes.

How The Bee Became

Now in the middle of the earth lived a demon. This demon spent all his time groping about in the dark tunnels, searching for precious metals and gems.

He was hunch-backed and knobbly-armed. His ears draped over his shoulders like a wrinkly cloak. These kept him safe from the bits of rock that were always falling from the ceilings of his caves. He had only one eye, which was a fire. To keep this fire alive he had to feed it with gold and silver. Over this eye he cooked his supper every night. It is hard to say what he ate. All kinds of fungus that grew in the airless dark on the rocks. His drink was mostly of tar and oil, which he loved. There is no end of tar and oil in the middle of the earth.

He rarely came up to the light. Once, when he did, he saw the creatures that God was making.

'What's this?' he cried, when a grasshopper landed on his clawed, horny foot. Then he saw Lion. Then Cobra. Then, far above him, Eagle.

'My word!' he said, and hurried back down into his dark caves to think about what he had seen.

He was jealous of the beautiful things that God was making.

'I will make something,' he said at last, 'which will be far more beautiful than any of God's creatures.'

But he had no idea how to set about it.

So one day he crept up to God's workshop and watched God at work. He peeped from behind the door. He saw him model the clay, bake it in the sun's fire, then breathe life into it. So that was it!

Away he dived, back down into the centre of the earth.

At the centre of the earth it was too hot for clay. Everything was already baked hard. He set about trying to make his own clay.

First, he ground up stones between his palms. That was powder. But how was he to make it into clay? He needed water, and there in the centre of the earth it was too hot for water.

He searched and he searched, but there was none. At last he sat down. He felt so sad he began to cry. Big tears rolled down his nose.

'If only I had water,' he sobbed, 'this clay could become a real living creature. Why do I have to live where there is no water?'

He looked at the powder in his palm, and began to cry afresh. As he looked and wept, and looked and wept, a tear fell off the end of his nose straight into the powder.

But he was too late. A demon's tears are no ordinary tears. There was a red flash, a fizz, a bubbling, and where the powder had been was nothing but a dark stain on his palm.

He felt like weeping again. Now he had water, but no powder.

'So much for stone-powder,' he said. 'I need something stronger.'

Then quickly, before his tears dried, he ground some of the precious metal that he used to feed the fire in his eye. As soon as it was powder he wetted it with a tear off his cheek. But it was no better than the stone-powder had been. There was flash, a fizz, a bubbling, and nothing.

'Well,' he said. 'What now?'

At last he thought of it — he would make a powder of precious gems. It was hard work grinding these, but at last he had finished. Now for a tear. But he was too excited to cry. He struggled to bring up a single tear. It was no good. His eye was dry as an oven. He struggled and he struggled. Nothing! All at once he sat down and burst into tears.

'It's no good!' he cried. 'I can't cry!' Then he felt his tears wet on his cheeks.

'I'm crying!' he cried joyfully. 'Quick, quick!' And he splashed a tear on to the powder of the precious gems. The result was perfect. He had made a tiny piece of beautiful clay. Only tiny, because his tears had been few. But it was big enough.

'Now,' he said, 'what kind of creature shall I make?'

The jewel-clay was very hard to work into shape. It was tough as red-hot iron.

So he laid the clay on his anvil and began to beat it into shape with his great hammer.

He beat and beat and beat that clay for a thousand years.

And at last it was shaped. Now it needed baking. Very carefully, because the thing he had made was very frail, he put it into the fire of his eye to bake.

Then, beside a great heap of small pieces of gold and silver, for another thousand years he sat, feeding the fire of his eye with the precious metal. All this time, in the depths of his eye glowed his little creature, baking slowly.

At last it was baked.

Now came the real problem. How was he going to breathe life into it?

He puffed and he blew, but it was no good.

'It is so beautiful!' he cried. 'I must give it life!'

It certainly was beautiful. All the precious gems of which it was made mingled their colours. And from the flames in which it had been baked, it had taken a dark fire. It gleamed and flashed: red, blue, orange, green, purple, no bigger than your finger-nail.

But it had no life.

There was only one thing to do. He must go to God and ask him to breathe life into it.

When God saw the demon he was amazed. He had no idea that such a creature existed.

'Who are you?' he asked. 'Where have you come from?'

The demon hung his head. 'Now,' he thought, 'I will use a trick.'

'I'm a jewel-smith,' he said humbly. 'And I live in the centre of the earth. I have brought you a present, to show my respect for you.'

He showed God the little creature that he had made. God was amazed again.

'How beautiful!' he kept saying as he turned it over and over in his hand. 'How beautiful! What a wonderfully clever smith you are.'

'Ah!' said the demon. 'But not so clever as you. I could never breathe life into it. If you had made it, it would be alive. As it is, it is beautiful, but dead.'

God was flattered. 'That's soon altered,' he said. He raised the demon's gift to his lips and breathed life into it.

Then he held it out. It crawled on to the end of his finger.

'Buzz!' it went, and whirred its thin, beautiful wings.

Like a flash, the demon snatched it from God's finger-tips and plunged back down into the centre of the earth.

There, for another thousand years, he lay, letting the little creature crawl over his fingers and make short flights from one hand to the other. It glittered all its colours in the light of his eye's fire. The demon was very happy.

'You are more beautiful than any of God's creatures,' he crooned.

But life was hard for the little creature down in the centre of the earth, with no one to play with but the demon. He had God's breath in him, and he longed to be among the other creatures under the sun.

And he was sad for another reason. In his veins ran not blood, but the tears with which the demon had mixed his clay. And what is sadder than a tear? Feeling the sadness in all his veins, he moved restlessly over the demon's hands.

One day the demon went up to the light to compare his little creature with the ones God had made.

'Buzz!' went his pet, and was away over a mountain.

'Come back!' roared the demon, then quickly covered his mouth with his hands, frightened that God would hear him. He began to search for his creature, but soon, frightened that God would see him, he crept back into the earth.

Still his little creature was not happy.

The sadness of the demon's tears was always in him. It was part of him. It was what flowed in his veins.

'If I gather everything that is sweet and bright and happy,' he said to himself, 'that should make me feel better. Here there are plenty of wonderfully sweet bright happy things.'

And he began to fly from flower to flower, collecting the bright sunny sweetness out of their cups.

'Ah!' he cried. 'Wonderful!'

The sweetness lit up his body. He felt the sun glowing through him from what he drank. For the first time in his life he felt happy.

But the moment he stopped drinking from the flowers, the sadness came creeping back along his veins and the gloom into his thoughts.

'That demon made me of tears,' he said. 'How can I ever hope to get away from the sadness of tears? Unless I never leave these flowers.'

And he hurried from flower to flower.

He could never stop, and it was too good to stop.

Soon, he had drunk so much, the sweetness began to ooze out of his pores. He was so full of it, he was brimming over with it. And every second he drank more.

At last he had to pause.

'I must store all this somewhere,' he said.

So he made a hive, and all the sweetness that oozed from him he stored in that hive. Man found it and called it honey. God saw what the little creature was doing, and blessed him, and called him Bee.

But Bee must still go from flower to flower, seeking sweetness. The tears of the demon are still in his veins ready to make him gloomy the moment he stops drinking from the flowers. When he is angry and stings, the smart of his sting is the tear of the demon. If he has to keep that sweet, it is no wonder that he drinks sweetness until he brims over.

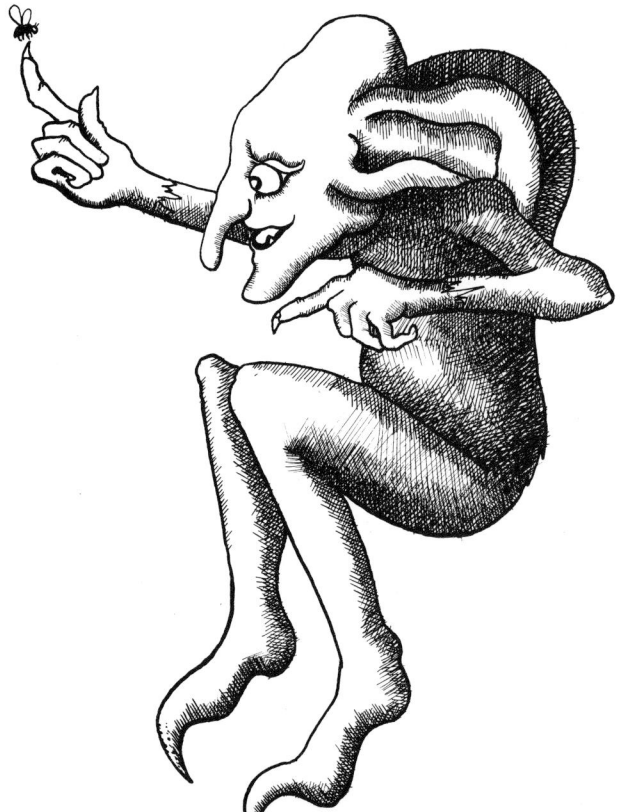

To think and talk about

A   1.   The demon decided to make a creature more beautiful than any of God's creatures. Did he decide this quickly?

      2.   'If only I had water, this clay would become a living creature.' Was the demon right?

      3.   Why was the demon's creature beautiful?

      4.   Does the demon feel he has succeeded in his desire?

      5.   What cures Bee's sadness?

B   1.   Do you think the demon is a wicked demon?

      2.   What do you think God thinks of the demon?

      3.   How does the demon feel about the creatures God is making?

      4.   Why do you think the demon could not breathe life into his creature?

      5.   Is this a story you could believe?

      6.   Do you think God was really tricked?

More books to read

1. *Meet My Folks* by Ted Hughes
   Eight funny and fantastic poems describing a family which you might like to have living near you.

2. *Comet in Moominland* by Tove Jansson
   Moomins are short and fat and shy and put everyone they meet under their spell. If you enjoy this book there are several others in the series.

3. *The Kingdom Under the Sea* by Joan Aiken
   Magic trees, carpets, and a frightening witch are found in this collection of stories. There are eleven stories so why not dip in and see how you like them?

Ideas to write about

Imagine that you are asked to be the 'eyes' of a blind person.
They have never seen a bee, and never will.
Describe the bee, so that they will get an idea of what it is like.

Searching for missing words

In the story below some words have been missed out.
Can you be sure which words have been missed out?
Sometimes there can be only one answer.
Sometimes there can be several answers for you to think and talk about.
How many words can you find?

This cottage always puzzled me. It had been empty for years. But the roof was in good condition; there was _____ in all the windows, and behind them lace _____ still hung primly. The door stood ajar, and _____ the orchard around was choked with weeds, the _____ up to the door was trodden down, as _____ someone went backwards and forwards regularly.

Inside the _____ was empty of furniture, but still dry and _____, and in the autumn, apples and plums ripened and _____, and nobody was there to gather them. Nobody _____ me, that is. Because I often walk along _____ way for curiosity's sake and for the plums.

_____ day on my way back from school, I _____ down to the cottage from the _____ above, and found someone there before me.

From *Mulroy's Magic* by Marjorie-Ann Watts

In the bee factory

It is night in the factory
where bees make bees,
always night and little sleep,
all the long hot summer through.

All the long dark summer through,
cradle-builders
are steadily fixing
wax against wax,
for the Great Queen follows them,
stepping from rim to rim to drop
the right egg in the right cot —
she must not stop,
she cannot stop —
ten thousand cradles for making bees!

Back down the line
eggs begin hatching,
hungry grubs rising,
night-nurse bees bustling
with bee-milk to feed them,
worker babies
to work for the factory.

Fat little grubs grow,
shed their skins,
grow again
(up the line, now, new
eggs begin hatching)
until they reach the right size,
turn, and close their eyes.

Here lies the secret,
the pride of our factory —
go to sleep maggot,
wake all bee!
Shiny legs, glossy wings,
stripy backs, stings —

success every time —
thousands the same!
Fresh for the work ahead,
hard work till they're dead.

Ah but the work's
out in the brightness —
up from the factory gate they rise
in haze of colours and sun humming,

the sweetest flowers to search for,
tastes to trace, sisters to tell,
gathering pollen and nectar, for honey
to feed the dark factory
where bees make bees
to fly in the brightness
gathering nectar
and pollen, for honey
to feed the dark factory
and make bees.

Libby Houston

What are they saying?

Look at what is happening in this picture.
What do you think the two people might be saying?

Is it in the picture?

Here are some sentences about the picture opposite.
Put them into three groups:

(a) True
(b) Untrue
(c) We cannot be sure

1. The road has a modern surface.

2. The fruit was brought to the market in the early morning.

3. The market is situated in a modern city.

4. The hikers are going to buy some fruit for their journey.

5. Only fruit and vegetables are sold in this market.

6. There is only one person buying and only one person serving at the stalls.

7. The large brown building is probably a hotel.

8. Cars are not allowed into this square.

9. Most of the stalls have no cover if it rains.

10. The cone shaped tower on the brown building has a painted pattern on its roof.

Ideas to talk about

In the story, God and the demon were making creatures.
We cannot make living things, but many people make things,
either as a job, or as a hobby.
Talk about something special you have made or helped make. It
might be a model, or a cake, or perhaps you have helped an adult
to build a garage or build furniture.
Describe how you made the thing, how successful you were, and
how you felt at the end.

Apostrophes

We are going to the cinema tonight.

We don't usually say it that way, do we?
We say:

We're going to the cinema tonight.

We put in the mark ' instead of the a. It is called the *apostrophe*.
How could you shorten the following?

she is   **you are**   **they are**

What do these shortened forms mean?
For example: **isn't** means **is not**

we've   **he'd**   **she'll**
you've   **I'm**   **wouldn't**

Reading for the main idea

The Journey

It took the travellers a long time to make their way through the forest. Often there was no real path to follow and they found themselves going in the wrong direction. Crossing wide streams was rather a problem and going through marshy ground was tiring. Their feet kept sinking up to their ankles in the soft ground. Thorns tugged at their clothing and leafy twigs flicked into their faces. It was a sorry group who, at last, reached their resting place for the night — a small inn where the landlord made them very welcome.

Stephen made notes of the main ideas in the story. Here is what he wrote:

- **travellers in a forest**
- **no path so they went in wrong direction.**

Think of the other main ideas.
Add them to Stephen's list so that you have notes on all the main ideas.
Talk about the notes you have made.
Does everyone agree about the main ideas?

Making words

How many new words can you make, using only letters found in

ANTARCTIC?

Sort it out

1. Here is a group of sentences which make a story.
   They are in the wrong order.
   Can you write the story in the correct order?

   (a) Father, however, was two hours late getting here, because the snow made driving difficult.

   (b) The children were very happy to see the thick blanket of snow.

   (c) The following morning the snow had turned to rain and the thaw had set in.

   (d) After two hours there was a covering of about five centimetres.

   (e) The snow soon started to cover the ground.

   (f) It had been cloudy all morning and at about two o'clock when we looked out we saw the first few flakes of snow.

2. The next set of sentences is more difficult.
   If you arrange them in the order in which they were written, and then take the second word from each sentence, these will make another sentence about the story.

   (a) 'It's super so far, Miss,' shouted one boy as he sat down.

   (b) They had breakfast early and then waited at the hotel entrance.

   (c) 'We're there,' thought Miss Summers, confident that the children would enjoy the trip she had spent so long planning.

   (d) Because everyone was excited, few of the children slept well.

   (e) Soon a coach came, and they all got on.

   (f) 'What time is lunch?' asked another as the coach set off for the city.

44

The game of life

Have you been in sight of heaven
Far ahead on ninety-seven
Then swirled the dice and thrown a one,
Slid down a snake and flopped upon
Some square like sixty-three?

And then what made you even madder
Seen your sister climb a ladder
To eighty-four from twenty-eight
And felt a sudden rush of hate
As she smirked with glee?

And have you thought she counted out
(So as to miss a snake's dread snout)
A few too many squares — and stayed
Quiet because you were afraid
Or just through leniency?

If so, you will already know
How bitter life can be; and show
Upon your countenance no sign
Except perhaps a smile benign.
And shake on doggedly.

Roy Fuller

Act it out

Josie's group played a miming game.
First the children had to decide on something to mime.
They started with **frying an egg**.
Josie mimed the actions she would go through when frying an egg.

The others watched to see if she made any mistakes.
Rick noticed that she forgot to switch on the cooker, so then it was his turn to try. When Rick tried the mime, Jan noticed he forgot to put the frying pan on the cooker.

Then it was Jan's turn.

After four people had tried frying an egg in mime, the group changed to **washing up** to continue the game.

Why not try playing this miming game?
Here are some ideas you might use:
> **sewing on a button**
> **peeling potatoes**
> **polishing shoes**
> **wrapping a parcel**

How well can you mime?
Watch each other in turn to see if all the detail is mimed.
Can you see any detail missing?

Here is a poem written by Janice, aged 10, about a mouse.

Mouse

Silk furred squeaker,
Pink nosed cheese eater.
Sits in the corner and looks.
Are you praying?
From the way you hold your paws,
I think you are.

Could you write a similar poem, entitled 'Bee'?

The company words keep

The children in Ruth's class were asked to think of as many
words as they could which meant roughly the same as **short**.
Here are their answers:

brief	**stocky**	**puny**
stubby	**dumpy**	**tiny**
little	**curt**	**not enough**

Can you see why these words might mean the same as **short**?

Do the same for these words.
Who can write down the most?

fierce	**wet**	**rich**

Now try these words:

spend	**enjoy**	**break**

Talk about the answers you have given.

The way words are built

Tele is an Ancient Greek word meaning 'far'.
How many words can you think of beginning with **tele** meaning 'far'? The first one is done for you.

telescope

Cent is from an old Roman word meaning 'one hundred'.
How many words can you find which begin with **cent**, meaning 'one hundred'? The first one is done for you.

centipede

unus   **duo**   **tres**

These are the old Roman words for one, two, and three.
How many words can you find beginning with each?
These are more difficult as they change their form slightly. Here are three examples:

unus (one) **unit**   **duo** (two) **duet**   **tres** (three) **triangle**

Using a dictionary might help.

UNIT 16

James lived with his two cruel aunts and was unhappy. One day he met an old man who gave him a bag of magic green things. James was excited, tripped, and fell beside the peach tree, and the green things escaped into the ground.

Soon a peach on the tree began to grow and grow till it was huge. James made his way into the peach where he met a gigantic Silkworm, a huge Ladybird, a great Centipede, an enormous Grasshopper, an outsize Spider and a big, fat Earthworm.

This is a story about one of the adventures James and his new friends had in the Giant Peach.

This story is taken from a book called *James and the Giant Peach* by Roald Dahl.

The great escape

'There *is something* that I believe we might try,' James Henry Trotter said slowly. 'I'm not saying it'll work . . .'

'Tell us!' cried the Earthworm. 'Tell us quick!'

'We'll try anything you say!' said the Centipede. 'But hurry, hurry, hurry!'

'Be quiet and let the boy speak!' said the Ladybird. 'Go on, James.'

They all moved a little closer to him. There was a longish pause.

'*Go on!*' they cried frantically. '*Go on!*'

And all the time while they were waiting they could hear the sharks threshing around in the water below them. It was enough to make anyone frantic.

'Come on, James,' the Ladybird said, coaxing him.

'I . . . I . . . I'm afraid it's no good after all,' James murmured, shaking his head. 'I'm terribly sorry. I forgot. We don't have any string. We'd need hundreds of yards of string to make this work.'

'What sort of string?' asked the Old-Green-Grasshopper sharply.

'Any sort, just so long as it's strong.'

'But my dear boy, that's exactly what we do have! We've got all you want!'

'How? Where?'

'The Silkworm!' cried the Old-Green-Grasshopper. 'Didn't you ever notice the Silkworm? He's still downstairs! He never moves! He just lies there sleeping all day long, but we can easily wake him up and make him spin!'

'And what about me, may I ask?' said Miss Spider. 'I can spin *just* as well as any Silkworm. What's more, *I* can spin patterns.'

'Can you make enough between you?' asked James.

'As much as you want.'

'And quickly?'

'Of course! Of course!'

'And would it be strong?'

'The strongest there is! It's as thick as your finger! But why? What are you going to do?'

'I'm going to lift this peach clear out of the water!' James announced firmly.

'You're mad!' cried the Earthworm.

'It's our only chance.'

'The boy's crazy!'

'He's joking!'

'Go on, James,' the Ladybird said gently. 'How are you going to do it?'

'Skyhooks, I suppose,' jeered the Centipede.

'Seagulls,' James answered calmly. 'The place is full of them. Look up there!'

They all looked and saw a great mass of seagulls wheeling round and round in the sky.

'I'm going to take a long silk string,' James went on, 'and I'm going to loop one end of it round a seagull's neck. And then I'm going to tie the other end to the stem of the peach.' He pointed to the peach stem, which was standing up like a short thick mast in the middle of the deck.

'Then I'm going to get another seagull and do the same thing again, then another and another —'

'Ridiculous!' they shouted.

'Absurd!'

'Poppycock!'

'Balderdash!'

'Madness!'

And the Old-Green-Grasshopper said, 'How can a few seagulls lift an enormous thing like this up into the air, and all of us as well? It would take hundreds . . . thousands . . .'

'There is no shortage of seagulls,' James answered. 'Look for yourself. We'll probably need four hundred, five hundred, six hundred . . . maybe even a thousand . . . I don't know . . . I shall simply go on hooking them up to the stem until we have enough to lift us. They'll be bound to lift us in the end. It's like balloons. You give someone enough balloons to hold, I mean *really* enough, then up he goes. And a seagull has far more lifting power than a balloon. If only we have the *time* to do it. If only we are not sunk first by those awful sharks . . .'

'You're absolutely off your head!' said the Earthworm.

'How on earth do you propose to get a loop of string round a seagull's neck? I suppose you're going to fly up there yourself and catch it!'

'The boy's dotty!' said the Centipede.

'Let him finish,' said the Ladybird. 'Go on, James. How *would* you do it?'

'With bait.'

'Bait! What sort of bait?'

'With a worm, of course. Seagulls love worms, didn't you know that? And luckily for us, we have here the biggest, fattest, pinkest, juiciest Earthworm in the world.'

'You can stop right there!' the Earthworm said sharply. 'That's quite enough!'

'Go on,' the others said, beginning to grow interested. 'Go on!'

'The seagulls have already spotted him,' James continued. 'That's why there are so many of them circling round. But they daren't come down to get him while all the rest of us are standing here. So this is what —'

'Stop!' cried the Earthworm. 'Stop, stop, stop! I won't have it! I refuse! I—I—I—I—'

'Be quiet!' said the Centipede. 'Mind your own business!'

'I *like* that!'

'My dear Earthworm, you're going to be eaten anyway, so what different does it make whether it's sharks or seagulls?'

'I won't do it!'

'Why don't we hear what the plan is first?' said the Old-Green-Grasshopper.

'I don't give a hoot what the plan is!' cried the Earthworm. 'I am not going to be pecked to death by a bunch of seagulls!'

'You will be a martyr,' said the Centipede. 'I shall respect you for the rest of my life.'

'So will I,' said Miss Spider. 'And your name will be in all the newspapers. Earthworm gives life to save friends ...'

'But he won't *have* to give his life,' James told them. 'Now listen to me. This is what we'll do ...'

'Why, it's absolutely brilliant!' cried the Old-Green-Grasshopper when James had explained his plan.

'The boy's a genius!' the Centipede announced. 'Now I can keep my boots on after all.'

'Oh, I shall be pecked to death!' wailed the poor Earthworm.

'Of course you won't.'

'I will, I know I will! And I won't even be able to see them coming at me because I have no eyes!'

James went over and put an arm gently round the Earthworm's shoulders. 'I won't let them *touch* you,' he said. 'I promise I won't. But we've *got* to hurry! Look down there!'

There were more sharks than ever now around the peach. The water was boiling with them. There must have been ninety or a hundred at least. And to the travellers up on top, it certainly seemed as though the peach were sinking lower and lower into the water.

'Action stations!' James shouted. 'Jump to it! There's not a moment to lose!' He was the captain now, and everyone knew it. They would do whatever he told them.

'All hands below deck except Earthworm!' he ordered.

'Yes, yes!' they said eagerly as they scuttled into the tunnel entrance. 'Come on! Let's hurry!'

'And you — Centipede!' James shouted. 'Hop downstairs and get that Silkworm to work at once! Tell him to spin as he's never spun before! Our lives depend upon it! And the same applies to you, Miss Spider! Hurry on down! Start spinning!'

In a few minutes everything was ready.

It was very quiet now on the top of the peach. There was nobody in sight — nobody except the Earthworm.

One half of the Earthworm, looking like a great, thick, juicy, pink sausage, lay innocently in the sun for all the seagulls to see.

The other half of him was dangling down the tunnel.

James was crouching close beside the Earthworm in the tunnel entrance, just below the surface, waiting for the first seagull. He had a loop of silk string in his hands.

The Old-Green-Grasshopper and the Ladybird were further down the tunnel, holding onto the Earthworm's tail, ready to pull him quickly in out of danger as soon as James gave the word.

And far below, in the great stone of the peach, the Glow-worm

54

was lighting up the room so that the two spinners, the Silkworm and Miss Spider, could see what they were doing. The Centipede was down there too, exhorting them both frantically to greater efforts, and every now and again James could hear his voice coming up faintly from the depths, shouting, 'Spin, Silkworm, spin, you great fat lazy brute! Faster, faster, or we'll throw you to the sharks!'

'Here comes the first seagull!' whispered James. 'Keep still now, Earthworm. Keep still. The rest of you get ready to pull.'

'Please don't let it spike me,' begged the Earthworm.

'I won't, I won't, Ssshhh ...'

Out of the corner of one eye, James watched the seagull as it came swooping down towards the Earthworm. And then suddenly it was so close that he could see its small black eyes and its curved beak, and the beak was open, ready to grab a nice piece of flesh out of the Earthworm's back.

'Pull!' shouted James.

The Old-Green-Grasshopper and the Ladybird gave the Earthworm's tail an enormous tug, and like magic the Earthworm disappeared into the tunnel. At the same time, up went James's hand and the seagull flew right into the loop of silk that he was holding out. The loop, which had been cleverly made, tightened just the right amount (but not too much) around its neck, and the seagull was captured.

'Hooray!' shouted the Old-Green-Grasshoper, peering out of the tunnel. 'Well done, James!'

Up flew the seagull with James paying out the silk string as it went. He gave it about fifty yards and then tied the string to the stem of the peach.   'Next one!' he shouted, jumping back into the tunnel. 'Up you get again, Earthworm! Bring up some more silk, Centipede!'

'Oh, I don't like this at all,' wailed the Earthworm. 'It only just missed me! I even felt the wind on my back as it went swishing past!'

'Ssshh!' whispered James. 'Keep still! Here comes another one!'

So they did it again.

And again, and again, and again.

And the seagulls kept coming, and James caught them one after the other and tethered them to the peach stem.

'One hundred seagulls!' he shouted, wiping the sweat from his face.

'Keep going!' they cried. 'Keep going, James!'

'Two hundred seagulls!'

'Three hundred seagulls!'

'Four hundred seagulls!'

The sharks, as though sensing that they were in danger of losing their prey, were hurling themselves at the peach more furiously than ever, and the peach was sinking lower and lower still in the water.

'Five hundred seagulls!' James shouted.

'Silkworm says he's running out of silk!' yelled the Centipede from below. 'He says he can't keep it up much longer. Nor can Miss Spider!'

'Tell them they've *got* to!' James answered. 'They can't stop now!'

'We're lifting!' somebody shouted.

'No, we're not!'

'I felt it!'

'Put on another seagull, quick!'

'Quiet, everybody! Quiet! Here's one coming now!'

This was the five hundred and first seagull, and the moment that James caught it and tethered it to the stem with all the others, the whole enormous peach suddenly started rising up slowly out of the water.

'Look out! Here we go! Hold on, boys!'

But then it stopped.

And there it hung.

It hovered and swayed, but it went no higher.

The bottom of it was just touching the water. It was like a delicately balanced scale that needed only the tiniest push to tip it one way or the other.

'One more will do it!' shouted the Old-Green-Grasshopper, looking out of the tunnel. 'We're almost there!'

And now came the big moment. Quickly, the five hundred and second seagull was caught and harnessed to the peach-stem ...

And then suddenly ...

But slowly ...

Majestically ...

Like some fabulous golden balloon ...

With all the seagulls straining at the strings above ...

The giant peach rose up dripping out of the water and began climbing towards the heavens.

To think and talk about

A 1. Which creatures seemed to do very little work?

2. Why do you think the other animals listened to James?

3. Why was the Earthworm not very keen on the plan? Do you think he is a coward?

4. From this story what do we learn about seagulls?

5. What might have caused James's plan to fail?

6. Who do you think had the most important job? Why?

B 1. If you were the Earthworm would you have agreed to the plan?

2. All the animals had a part to play. Which part would you prefer to play? Why?

3. How do you think the peach and the animals grew so big in the first place?

4. Look at what the Centipede says. Say what you think he is like. Do you like him?

5. Can you say why you liked or did not like this story?

Making words

How many new words can you make, using only letters found in

RHINOCEROS?

More books to read

1. *Danny, the Champion of the World* by Roald Dahl
   The amazing story of Danny and his father outwitting their greedy, rich neighbour. You're bound to laugh at their adventures.

2. *Fattypuffs and Thinifers* by André Maurois
   Edmund was fat. His brother Terry was thin. That was all right until they were in the underground kingdom. Fattypuffs were on the opposite side to Thinifers in a war!

3. *Log of the Ark* by Geoffrey Boumphrey and Kenneth Walker
   The story of Noah's journeys in the ark with the animals. You should find this an amusing book to read.

What are they saying?

Look at what is happening in this picture.
What do you think they might be saying?

The Ladybird

Tiniest of turtles
Your shining back
Is a shell of orange
With spots of black.

How trustingly you walk
Across this land
Of hairgrass and hollows
That is my hand.

Your small wire legs
So frail, so thin,
Their touch is swansdown
Upon my skin.

There, break out
Your wings and fly.
No tenderer creature
Beneath the sky.

Clive Sansom

Searching for missing words

In the story below some words have been missed out.
Can you be sure which words have been missed out?
Sometimes there can be only one answer.
Sometimes there can be several answers for you to think and talk about.
How many words can you find?

'Now I'll have a bite,' said Karp and took the rye-bread and the dried reindeer-meat from his birchbark satchel. He found he was extremely hungry, but he remembered to keep a piece of bread for Little Breadeater.

Presently he _____ he had better be off. He was a _____ way from home and he was not _____ sure which way to go. Even though _____ had come, he eyed the brooding forest _____. Everything seemed so silent and watchful.

He _____ better once he had harnessed Little Breadeater _____ was driving along again, watching that everlasting _____ on the reindeer's tail patch bobbing up and _____ and listening to the clickety-click-click of her _____ hooves and the tiny, hollow music of the _____ at her throat.

From *The Magic Bullet* by Alan Jenkins

Points of view

Here are a few facts about an incident which takes place in an auction room.

The Auction

A Welsh grocer decides to sell a painting which has hung in his sitting room for years. He takes it to an auction and expects to get about ten pounds.

Before the auction, a crowd begins to gather round his painting. The grocer thinks nothing of it and goes out for a drink and a chat with his friends. He arrives back just as his painting is put up for bids. He faints when the bids quickly pass ten thousand pounds. He eventually comes round in time to hear the painting going for the third and last time at fifteen thousand pounds. The grocer faints again.

Imagine you are

      (a) the grocer

or

      (b) the auctioneer

or

      (c) the buyer.

Could you give or write an account of the incident from your point of view?

Ideas to talk or write about

In 'The Great Escape' the Earthworm is called 'the fattest, pinkest, juiciest Earthworm in the world.'
Later he is called 'a great thick juicy pink sausage.'
These are good word pictures, aren't they?
Look back to the story.
Can you find any other word pictures about another creature?

Think about the Centipede
    its colour
    its body
    its expression

Can you build a word picture for the Centipede?
Now try another creature. Build another word picture.

Sort it out

1. Here is a group of sentences which make a story.
   They are in the wrong order.
   Can you write the story in the correct order?

   (a) Two small children were trapped in a bedroom.

   (b) Without waiting for the firemen she entered the house.

   (c) At about midnight she saw smoke coming from a house.

   (d) A policewoman was walking down the main street of a town.

   (e) The house was burned to the ground.

   (f) Without thinking of herself she rushed in and brought the boys out.

   (g) At once she radioed for help.

2. The next set of sentences is more difficult.
   If you arrange the sentences in the order in which they were first written, and then take the second word from each sentence, you will find another sentence about the story.

   (a) 'Look, instead of moaning, why don't you tidy your room?' suggested Mum, but at that moment the fault was fixed, and the programme restarted.

   (b) 'It's not gone again, has it? We had the man only last week,' answered Mum.

   (c) 'Very interesting, why don't they fix it instead of leaving the screen blank?' said Wanda.

   (d) 'Maybe something is wrong at the TV station,' said Dad.

   (e) 'Mum, why has the telly stopped working?' yelled Wanda.

   (f) 'Why do they always break down in the middle of my favourite programme?' moaned Wanda.

Check your facts

The Spider

As I sat resting, I saw that a spider was moving swiftly along the window ledge. It reached the end and continued down, onto the flower-patterned wall, to the skirting board. A chill overtook me as I watched. The spider was of the large black variety, which you sometimes see in houses, and often see enlarged into terrifying monsters in films. To kill it would be bad luck, and bring rain for a month of Mondays, as my mother had said. But I could not imagine sleeping here, with the possibility of that horror crawling into my bed. It was useless to tell myself that it would be more scared of me than I of it. But what was I to do?

Below are some sentences about the story.
Put them into three groups:
  (a) True
  (b) Untrue
  (c) We cannot be sure

1. The author intended to sleep in the room.

2. The author liked spiders.

3. The author would have to kill the spider.

4. The author was writing the story when he or she saw the spider.

5. The author had seen films with spider monsters.

6. The spider stopped at the end of the window sill.

7. The wall had a flower pattern on it.

8. The spider probably had a web in the corner.

9. The author was not sure what to do.

10. The author would be very tired in the morning.

Ideas to write about

1. Many people keep a diary of things that have happened to them. Here is a diary that one boy imagined about a journey of the Peach.

    3rd January 1988: Peachship. Captain James Henry Trotter reporting.
    Today we escaped the sharks.
    With our seagull friends we are going to an unknown destination.
    Crew Report
    Spider is complaining about the lack of juicy flies at this height.
    Centipede is sure he has frostbite in his rear twenty legs.

    Pretend that you are Captain Trotter. Write a diary of your journey through the sky. Think about the crew.

2. In the story 'The Great Escape' imagine the newpaper headlines after their escape . . .

    EARTHWORM RISKS LIFE TO SAVE FRIENDS

    Can you write a short report for a newspaper about it, and give a headline?
    To go with your report draw a picture of the Giant Peach just as it takes off.

3. Imagine you are the Earthworm.
    Describe how you feel about being used as bait.

Reading for the main idea

Justin was working on a project about the Romans and came across this passage in a book.

The Romans were so fond of bathing that they had public baths built in Rome which had many rooms and courtyards to cope with many bathers at one time. These baths were not places for swimming or washing in only. They were huge recreation centres with park, club, library, and concert hall included as facilities for the bathers. The bathing rooms were at varying temperatures. The first was gently heated. From there, bathers moved to the next which was hot, and the next which was even hotter. When the heat became too much they cooled themselves off in a huge open air pool called the *frigidarium*. Afterwards there were activities such as boxing, wrestling, and ball games. Beauty treatments could be enjoyed and while the people relaxed, refreshments were served.

Justin made notes of the main ideas in the story. Here is what he wrote:

Romans liked bathing
Rome had public baths.

Think of the other main ideas in the story. Add them to Justin's list so that you have notes of all the main ideas.
Can you use your notes to write a short piece based on the passage?

Act it out

Lorne's group thought each of the creatures in the story, 'The Great Escape', should have its own special voice. They talked about this idea. Here is some of what they said.

Lorne: The Green-Grasshopper ought to chatter.
Alison: Yes, but in a rustling sort of way, you know, as if he was a real grasshopper.
Ria: That sounds hard to do. But what about the Spider? I think he ought to be sinister, sort of slow and deep.
Lorne: Yes, I like that. What about the Silkworm? I think . . .

Well, what about the Silkworm? How would it speak?
Do you agree with what the children said about the voices?
What do you think?
Can you speak with the sort of voice you think each of the creatures should have?
Which one do you think you do best?
Why not try to imagine you are that creature, and tell the story of your escape, using the correct voice.

Wishes

Suppose you won a lot of money.
What would you do? Why?

Here is a shape poem about an earthworm.

Earthworm

Do
you
squirm
when
you
see
an earthworm?
I never
do squirm
because I think
a big fat worm
is really rather clever
the way it can shrink
and go
so small
without
a sound
into the ground.
And then
what about
all
that
work it does
and no oxygen
or miner's hat?
Marvellous
you have to admit
even if you don't like fat
pink worms a bit
how with that
thin
slippery skin
it makes its way
day after day
through the soil,
such honest toil.

                And don't forget
                 the dirt
              it eats, I bet
you wouldn't like to come out
    at night to squirt
       it all over the place
with no eyes in your face.
            I doubt
              too if you know
               an earthworm is deaf, but
          it can hear *you* go
         to and fro
even if you cut
 it in half.
   So
   do not laugh
    or squirm
     again
      when
        you
          suddenly
            see
            a worm.

                    Leonard Clark

Do you like the poem about the earthworm?
Could you write a shape poem about one of the other animals in
the story?
Remember the shape of the animal when you are writing your
poem.
Would it be better to draw the shape first?

The company words keep

Sounds

There are lots or words which tell you about sounds.
In 'The Great Escape' it says
   '. . . they could hear the sharks **threshing** around in the water
below them.'
   'I . . . I . . . I'm afraid it's no good after all,' James **murmured** . . .

    threshing   **murmured**

Can you find any more *sound* words in the story?

How many *sound* words can you think of that would describe
these pictures.

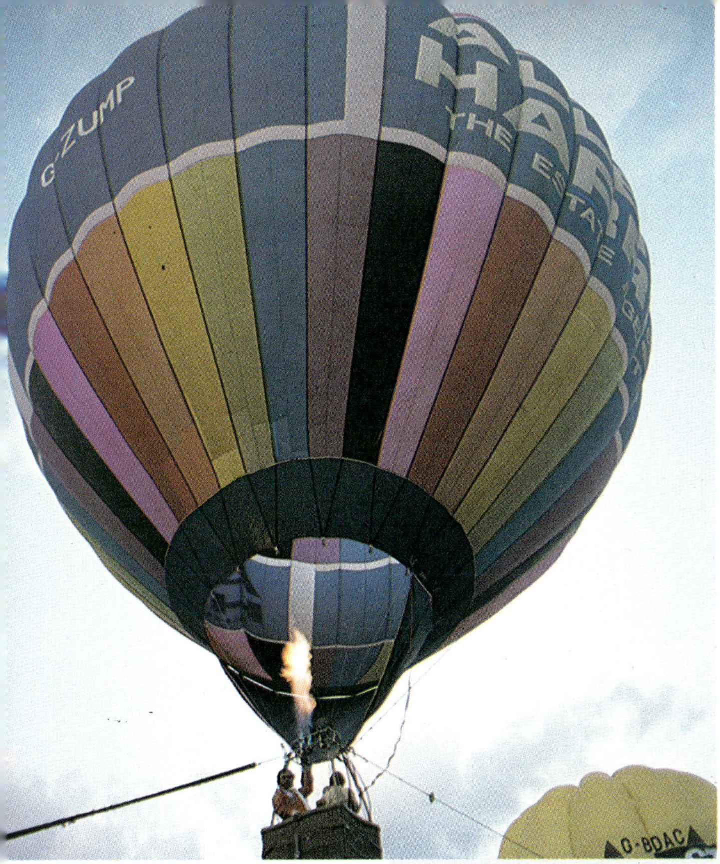
G-ZUMP
G-BDAC

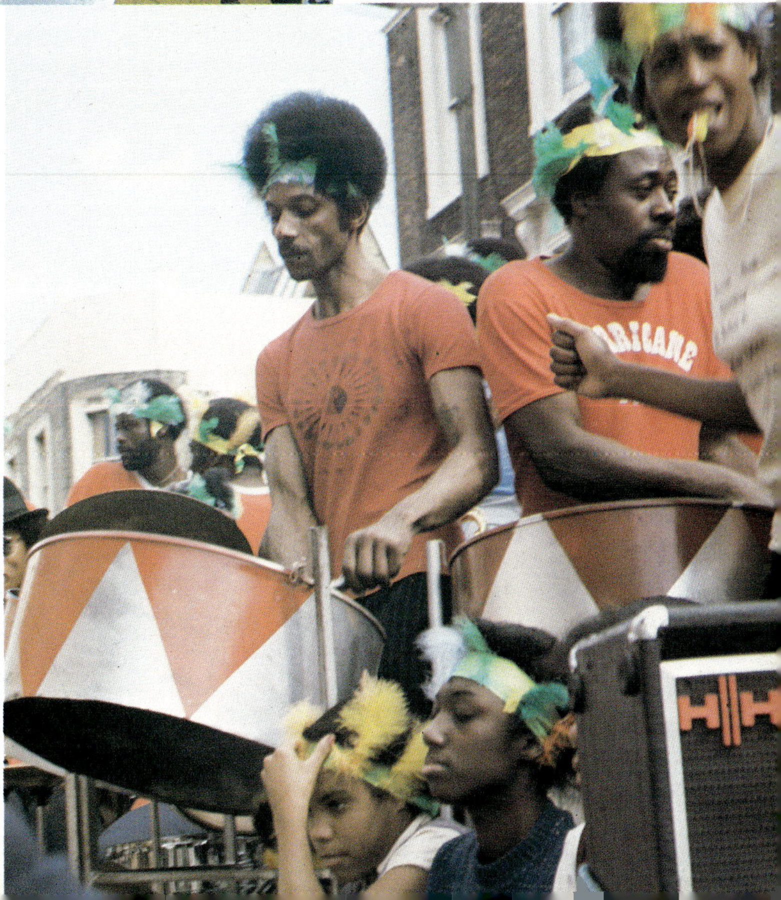

Apostrophes

Jack   **The dog which belongs to Jack**

If we talk or write about the dog which belongs to Jack, we usually say

Jack's dog

Can you alter each sentence below, so that it has a part in it like 'Jack's dog'? The first one is done for you.

1. Jean has a new dress, which is blue.
   Answer: Jean's new dress is blue.

2. Father has a new pipe, but it is broken.

3. My car has a buckled wheel.

4. The tramp had a very old hat.

5. My rabbit has long silky ears.

6. The cow had bent horns.

7. A nurse does a very valuable job.

8. Yesterday we visited the house where Joan lives.

9. The lion had a sore paw.

10. The ship had a broken rudder.

Ideas to talk about

The Peach is surrounded by sharks!
Can you describe the scene? Look back at the picture on page 56.
Some of the things you could talk about are

the sea
the sharks
the seagulls
the noises you hear
the appearance of the Peach.

Crossword

Can you make up clues for this crossword?

¹r	h	²y	m	³e
a	■	o	■	v
⁴d	o	u	s	e
i	■	r	■	n
⁵o	u	s	t	s

Across

1.

4.

5.

Down

1.

2.

3.

The way words are built

The names of streets in towns are often very interesting. They can tell a lot about the history of the town if you think about them. The two street names below tell us about trades which were carried on in the town many years ago. What do you think they were?

FURNACE ROAD

LEATHER LANE

Here are some more street names, some of which you might find locally. Talk about them and what the reasons may be for their names.

Corn Street
Church Street
Downing Street
London Road
Barrack Street
Tithebarn Street
Canal Street

King's Stables Road
Comely Bank Road
Saltmarket
Peep O' Day Lane
Pudding Lane
Glover Street
Quarry Steps

Do you know of streets or roads near your school with interesting or unusual names? How do you think these came about?

Rebecca is a girl who has come through a telescope to a strange world. In the part of the story which follows, Rebecca and her strange looking friend, Grisby, find themselves being chased by terrifying ghosts.

The story is from the book called *Rebecca's World* by Terry Nation.

Chased by the Ghosts

It was very spooky.

A thick fog wrapped her in its cloudy billows. And the silence was so silent that it seemed to echo all around her. Rebecca blinked her eyes quickly to be certain she was seeing properly. She was.

The fog was pink. Pink fog.

'It's like being inside a ball of candy floss,' she thought.

She stretched an arm out in front of her and lost sight of it. She pulled it back quickly and was relieved to see her hand still attached. She groped her way forward for a pace or two. And then she heard the noise. A low sort of groaning, moaning sound that was really quite scary. And the worst thing about it was that it was coming closer.

Then she heard the footsteps. Shuffling, scuffling, slow footsteps. Rebecca strained to penetrate the candy floss fog, but could see nothing. The eerie sounds were coming closer.

Rebecca decided that even though the little man in the round room was not very nice, being inside with him was better than being outside on her own. She turned around and started for the door. But it wasn't there. At least if it was, she couldn't see it.

She took a few blind steps to the right. And then to the left. And then a few paces backwards, until finally she didn't know which way she was going. And all the time the moaning sound and the shuffling footsteps came nearer.

The creature, whatever it was, seemed very near now. The fog distorted the sound so much that it seemed to be coming from all around her.

'I'll be brave,' thought Rebecca. Then instantly changed her

78

mind and started to run.

She set out with the speed of a galloping racehorse, but had not taken more than three strides when she crashed into something large and soft and green. She hit it with such force that she bounced backwards, tripped over, and sat down hard. The large, soft, green thing gave a great bellow of pain.

Rebecca scrambled to her feet ready to dash off again, when the fog cleared a little and she had a chance to get a look at the 'creature'. It wasn't nearly so frightening as she had imagined.

On the ground in front of her was the most miserable man she had ever seen. His mouth turned down at the corners, his forehead wrinkled in a frown and his eyes seemed on the verge of tears. His voice was the saddest she had ever heard.

'Why can't you look where you're going?'

There was no anger in the voice. It was full of sorrow and self-pity.

'I'm very sorry,' said Rebecca. 'I was running away from you.'

'Mmmmm,' said the man. 'People do. They say I depress them.'

He limped a bit closer, groaning and grunting with every shuffling step. He was wearing a raggy, shaggy, green fur coat with a matching hat.

'I like your coat,' said Rebecca, hoping a compliment would cheer him up.

'Thank you,' he said. 'It's past its best though. It was brown when I got it, but it's got a bit mildewed. It's the fog that does it.' He took another step forward, wincing as he did.

'Is there something wrong with your feet? asked Rebecca.

'Something wrong with my feet?' he echoed. 'You may well ask. You may well ask if there's something wrong with my feet.'

'All right,' said Rebecca. 'Is there something wrong with your feet?'

The man pointed an accusing finger towards his feet.

'Those feet,' he said, 'are the most painful feet in the entire universe. Concentrated into those two extremities is a massive quantity of pure undiluted agony.' He talked about his feet as thought they belonged to somebody else.

'Those feet,' he went on, 'are the sorest pair of throbbers in the entire history of feet. Would you like to see them?'

'No thank you,' answered Rebecca. 'It's very kind of you to offer though.'

The man seemed more cheerful now he was talking about his feet.

'I don't blame you,' he said. 'I only look at them myself when I'm forced to. Between them,' he said, looking down at his boots, 'they have every foot ailment known to science. Corns. Callouses. Verrucas. Bunions. Fallen arches. Gout. Ingrowing and outgrowing toe nails. And some things the doctors haven't even found names for yet. Yes. They're throbbers. Real little throbbers. By the way. My name is Grisby.'

They shook hands.

'I'm Rebecca or Becky, or sometimes just Beck. Whichever you prefer.' She quite liked Grisby. He wasn't very cheerful but at least he was friendly.

'Going anywhere special?' asked Grisby.

'Nowhere in particular,' Rebecca answered.

'Oh good. That's where I'm going too. I'll limp along with you.'

And they started to walk. At least, Rebecca walked. Grisby just hobbled, grimacing with every step.

The candy floss fog was clearing now. They were in what seemed to be a park, with neat flower beds and gravel paths.

In the distance was what Rebecca supposed was a town, although the buildings were unlike any she had ever seen. All sweeping curves and gentle arcs and graceful spirals. They looked as if they were made from glass.

Then Rebecca noticed something else. There were no trees. Not one. She stared around in a full circle. There wasn't a tree in sight.

She was just going to ask Grisby about this when the silence was broken by the most dreadful shrieking screech Rebecca had ever heard. It rose to an ear-piercing peak, then faded for a moment, only to build up again still louder.

Grisby stopped dead in his tracks. His hands began to shake and his face went deathly pale. Even his fur coat seemed to go a shade lighter. His whole body trembled.

'What is it?' asked Rebecca nervously.

Grisby could hardly speak he seemed so frightened. Finally he managed to croak out: 'The GHOST warning. Come on. Run for your life!'

Grisby exploded into action. He started to run at a speed that astonished Rebecca. From the back he looked like a great, green, grizzly bear. He seemed to have forgotten about his feet completely. They were moving so fast that they vanished into a blur.

Rebecca sped after him. She managed to draw alongside.

'What are we running away from?' she gasped.

'The GHOSTS,' panted Grisby. 'Horrible evil monsters. If they catch us they'll take us away and do wicked things to us!'

He managed a nervous glance over his shoulder and gave a little gurgle.

'Here they come!' he said. And though it seemed impossible, he doubled his speed, travelling now like a flash of green lightning.

Rebecca turned to see what had so frightened Grisby.

Coming along the path behind them were . . . 'things'. There was no other word to describe them. One moment they looked as though they were made from grey jelly, the next they seemed to be billows of oily smoke. You could almost see right through them.

Their shape changed as they moved. First they were toweringly tall, then slinkingly short. Thin, then fat. They seemed to have neither arms nor legs, but despite that they were moving at great speed.

Rebecca wasn't sure whether she imagined it, but she thought she saw gaping red mouths and huge, sharp teeth. What she didn't imagine was that these were the most frightening things she had ever seen. They looked like shapeless pieces of a nightmare that had escaped into day.

Rebecca didn't stare for a moment longer than was necessary. Her legs moved so fast she couldn't feel her feet touching the ground. She and Grisby were running neck and neck, and both were so breathless and frightened that they couldn't speak.

They were approaching a point where another path crossed the one along which they were running. As they reached it, Grisby put out his right arm, then made a skidding turn to the left. Rebecca was so confused by this that she went on for several yards before she could stop and change direction. By which time Grisby had put a fair distance between them.

The GHOSTS were now catching up. The little mouse called fear was not only running up and down Rebecca's spine, it was also crawling across her scalp and making her hair stand on end.

Grisby seemed to be heading for a group of wooden buildings some distance ahead. Rebecca could see many other people running in the same direction. All fleeing in terror at the approach of the GHOSTS.

As she drew closer she could see that the other fugitives were running into a doorway in the centre of the largest wooden building. By the time Rebecca was close enough to see the place properly, everybody had vanished inside. Only she and Grisby were left running towards it.

Then Grisby reached the doorway, and he too disappeared.

Rebecca was alone now. The gaping black entrance was about ten yards ahead. She allowed herself a sigh of relief. She was nearly safe.

She was within one stride of the opening when, with frightening suddenness, the two great doors slammed shut in her face. She smashed into them with the force of a cannon ball, but was too scared to feel hurt. She banged on the door with her clenched fist.

'Let me in. Please let me in,' she yelled at the top of her voice. 'Please ... please, Grisby. Let me in.' But the doors stayed firmly closed.

Desperately, she turned around. The GHOSTS were less than a hundred yards away. They had spread out in a long line and were advancing slowly towards her. They were making a sort of hissing sound like ten million angry snakes. As they moved, they gave off a slithery noise.

They came closer and closer.

Rebecca looked swiftly to the right. There was nothing. To the left she saw there was a narrow opening between two of the buildings. She ran towards it, noticing there were no windows or openings of any kind in the wooden walls.

She darted into the gap and found herself in a narrow alleyway, flanked on each side by tall timber walls. Her footsteps echoed and clattered as she ran.

Behind her the first GHOST darkened the entrance. It oozed forward to follow her and the others slithered along behind it.

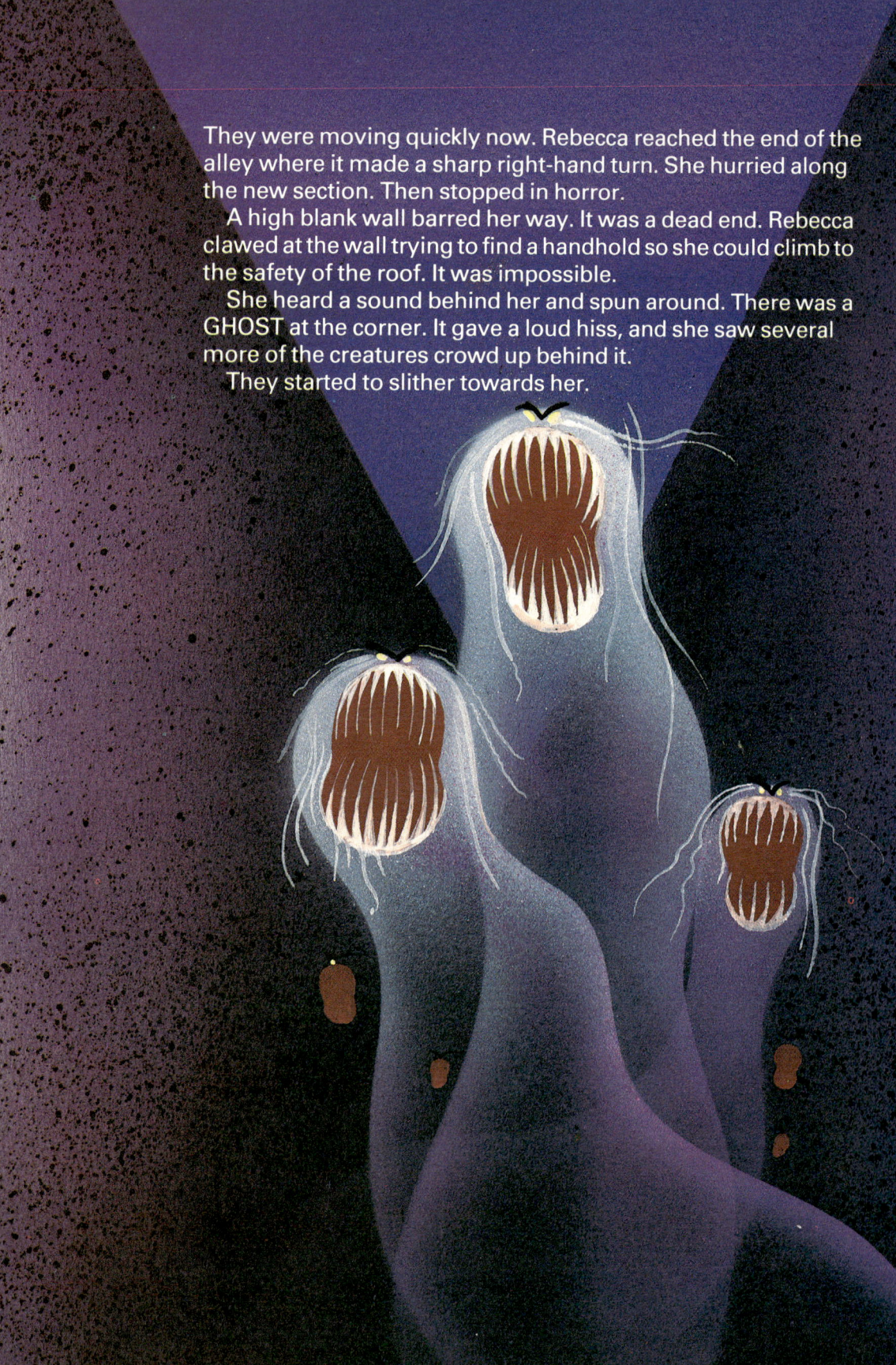

They were moving quickly now. Rebecca reached the end of the
alley where it made a sharp right-hand turn. She hurried along
the new section. Then stopped in horror.

A high blank wall barred her way. It was a dead end. Rebecca
clawed at the wall trying to find a handhold so she could climb to
the safety of the roof. It was impossible.

She heard a sound behind her and spun around. There was a
GHOST at the corner. It gave a loud hiss, and she saw several
more of the creatures crowd up behind it.

They started to slither towards her.

To think and talk about

A 1. What was the first thing about Grisby which struck Rebecca as being strange?
Why was it so strange?

2. What are all the things that are said about the shape of the ghosts?

3. How did the ghosts come down the alley?

4. How much noise do the ghosts make? How do you know? What seems to make them thrive?

5. Was Rebecca hurt when she hit the doors? How do you know?

B 1. Rebecca thought she saw gaping red mouths and huge sharp teeth. Can you find where it says this?
Read the paragraph again.
Now think and talk about this.
What do you think the other people saw, when they looked at the ghosts?

2. Do you think you would have liked Grisby? Why?

3. Why do you think there were no openings in the walls of the buildings?

4. What do you think the buildings were?

5. If you were the author, how would you get Rebecca out of the situation at the end of the story?

6. If *you* had been there instead of Rebecca, in what ways might things have been different? Would you have been afraid?

More books to read

1. *Charlotte Sometimes* by Penelope Farmer
   Join Charlotte as she goes back fifty years by changing places with a ghost of her own age!

2. *Anne of Green Gables* by L. M. Montgomery
   The story of Anne — a red-headed orphan — has been enjoyed by children for over fifty years.

3. *Space Hostages* by Nicholas Fisk
   Do you think you would be able to fly a spaceship? The children in this story find they have to when they are kidnapped.

Ideas to write about

1. The story 'Chased by the Ghosts', is about terror. To Rebecca, the Ghosts 'looked like shapeless pieces of a nightmare that had escaped into day'.
   Have you ever had a nightmare?
   Write a story called 'Nightmare'.

2. Imagine that you are one of the Ghosts.
   Write the story of the chase, as *you* see it.
   What are your feelings? What do you think of the people you are chasing, and trying to catch?

3. Imagine that Rebecca has come back to our world.
   You are a reporter, interviewing her about her unusual experiences.
   Decide on the questions you might ask, and then decide on the answers she would give.
   Write out the interview.

Searching for missing words

In the passage some words have been missed out.
Can you be sure which words have been missed out?
Sometimes there can be only one answer.
Sometimes there can be several answers for you to think and
talk about.
How many words can you find?

As soon as the first sunbeam touched him, the little ghost felt a
violent blow on the head, which almost threw him to the
ground. Crying out, he put his hands in front of his face and
began reeling about.

'Look, look!' cried the _____. 'What happened to the ghost?
It was _____ before, and now it has suddenly turned _____!
Black as a chimney sweep!'

The little _____ heard the children shouting, but he did
_____ understand what they were saying. He could _____
that something he could not explain had _____ to him. How
was he to know _____ ghosts turn black at the first touch
_____ a sunbeam?

'I must get away!' was his _____ clear thought. 'I must get
out of _____.'

But where could he go in all this _____?
Not back to the attic – the children _____ in the way.
The well in the _____ of the yard!

From *The Little Ghost* by Otfried Preussler

87

Here is a poem about a ghost visiting an old lady who had found a Hairy Toe.

The Hairy Toe

Once there was a woman went out to pick beans,
and she found a Hairy Toe.
She took the Hairy Toe home with her,
and that night, when she went to bed,
the wind began to moan and groan.
Away off in the distance
she seemed to hear a voice crying,
'Who's got my Hair-r-ry To-o-oe?
Who's got my Hair-r-ry To-o-oe?'
The woman scrooched down
'way under the covers,
and about that time
the wind appeared to hit the house,
smoosh,
and the old house creaked and cracked
like something was trying to get in.
The voice had come nearer,
almost at the door now,
and it said,
'Where's my Hair-r-y To-o-oe?
Who's got my Hair-r-ry To-o-oe?'
The woman scrooched further down
under the covers
and pulled them tight around her head.
The wind growled around the house
like some big animal
and r-r-um-mbled
over the chimbley.
All at once she heard the door cr-r-a-ack
and Something slipped in
and began to creep over the floor.

The floor went
cre-e-eak, cre-e-eak
at every step that thing took towards her bed.
The woman could almost feel
it bending over her bed.
Then in an awful voice it said:
'Where's my Hair-r-ry To-o-oe?
Who's got my Hair-r-ry To-o-oe?
You've got it!'

Traditional American Ballad

Points of view

Here are a few facts about a Pet Show.

The Pet Show

All the animals are lined up for judging. There are three beautiful dogs, two cats, a pony, a tortoise, a snake, a hairy caterpillar, a tame fox, two white rabbits, and several hamsters and white mice in the line up. The judges walk up and down the group asking questions and looking carefully at the animals. After great deliberation, the hairy caterpillar is awarded first prize. There is uproar amongst the crowd and contestants.

Imagine you are

    (a) one of the other contestants
or (b) one of the judges
or (c) the child who won the competition.

Could you give or write an account of the Pet Show from your point of view?

Funny words

What word do you think the artist has made a drawing of in this picture?

There are lots of words which are funny if you think about them. Talk about how you might make a funny drawing of the word

headstrong

Can you draw a picture for **headstrong**?

90

How to use a book

Bill's parents decided to go to London for a holiday. Bill wanted to go too, and his parents said they would take him to many famous places in the city.

Bill found a book in the library on London. It was very long and the only way he could look up the places he wanted to visit was to use the **index** at the back.

Here is part of the index from Bill's library book.

Paddington	123	Wembley	73
Parks	14–23	Westminster Abbey	27
Parliament, Houses of	84–85	Westminster Cathedral	28
Paul's, St (Cathedral)	69	Whittington, Dick	33
Restaurants	180–196	Whitehall	2
Shoreditch	62	Wimbledon	74
Thames, River	3	Wren, Christopher	61
Tower Bridge	19	Zoos	143–145
Twickenham	41		

1. Is the index in correct alphabetical order?

2. Can you tell which of the pages above deal with sport?

3. Which page would you look up if you wanted to
   (a) have a picnic?
   (b) find out about tennis?
   (c) see how large ships sail up-river?

They also bought a little book which gave a list of all the main shops in London. It helped them a lot.

Could you think of either roads or shops near you, and make a list of them just like an index?

Act it out

Do you know, there are stories which tell of people who have seen ghosts, and have been driven mad with terror?
How do you think you would feel if you really saw a ghost?
Perhaps you would run away, desperate for safety?
Or perhaps you would be rooted to the spot with fear?
What do you think you would do?
Can you imagine how you would feel if you told the story, and people would not believe you?
Try talking about this scene with some friends.

One of you has seen a ghost, and comes in terror to tell the others. But they will not believe you.

What happens?
What will make them believe?
Why not try acting the scene?

Crossword

Can you make up clues for this crossword?

¹c	o	²v	e	³r
l		o		u
⁴o	l	d	e	r
w		k		a
n		⁵a	i	l

Across

1.

4.

5.

Down

1.

2.

3.

To write about

This picture is part of a story.
Write the story into which you think it fits.

Fact or opinion?

What do *you* think a **fact** is?
What do *you* think an **opinion** is?

Sometimes in a passage facts and opinions are mixed up and it is helpful if we know the difference.
Here are some examples of facts and opinions for you to talk about.

1. The earth is round.   **fact**

2. Everyone loves summertime.   **opinion**

3. The capital of Britain is London.   **fact**

4. Sydney is an exciting city in which to live.   **opinion**

Here are some more sentences. Try to put them into two groups:
    (a) Facts
    (b) Opinions

1. Owls hunt at night.

2. Everyone enjoys swimming.

3. The owl is the most deadly night hunter.

4. London and Paris have underground railways.

5. Underground railways are the fastest means of transport in London and Paris.

6. Busy roads are dangerous places for young children.

Ideas to write about

Imagine that you are in Rebecca's world.
In the war with the Ghosts, you have to move a lot of wooden planks. But, to your horror, you find that the people have no carts, and have no idea what a cart is, or what one looks like. They do not even know what a wheel is.

How would you go about describing to these people, how to make a cart?

Reading for the main idea

Pamela was working on a project about a man called Houdini. She came across this passage in a book.

Even as a very young boy, Houdini was able to pick most types of lock. He decided to make a career of conjuring, centring his act around the art of escape. Whenever he set out to do a show in America he would experiment first by obtaining permission to be locked up in the strongest local police station cell from which he would attempt to escape. He usually succeeded in doing this within a matter of minutes, even though handcuffed into the bargain. Some of his most famous tricks included escaping from the inside of a packing case which was lowered beneath the surface of a river, wriggling out of a straitjacket while dangling from a skyscraper, or surviving being buried in a coffin below the ground. He became a legend all over the world and appeared in many short films.

Pamela made notes of the main ideas in the story. Here is what she wrote:

> — **Houdini — young — picks locks**
> — **decides to be conjurer.**

Think of other main ideas in the story. Add them to Pamela's list so that you have all the main ideas.
Can you use your notes to write your own shortened version of the story 'Houdini'?

Here is a poem about a strange creature from another planet who visits a school classroom.

The Marrog

My desk's at the back of the class
   And nobody, nobody knows
     I'm a Marrog from Mars
With a body of brass
   And seventeen fingers and toes.

Wouldn't they shriek if they knew
   I've three eyes at the back of my head
     And my hair is bright purple
My nose is deep blue
   And my teeth are half-yellow, half-red.

My five arms are silver, and spiked
   With knives on them sharper than spears.
I could go back right now, if I liked —
   And return in a million light–years.

I could gobble them all,
For I'm seven foot tall
   And I'm breathing green flames from my ears.

Wouldn't they yell if they knew,
    If they guessed that a Marrog was here?
Ha-ha, they haven't a clue —
    Or wouldn't they tremble with fear!
'Look, look a Marrog'
    They'd all scream — and SMACK
The blackboard would fall and the ceiling would crack
    And teacher would faint, I suppose.
But I grin to myself, sitting right at the back
    And nobody, nobody knows.

R. C. Scriven

Here is a poem called

Space

Slowly I float away
Peace and silence around me
Another world below me
Coming nearer to my view
Earth fades away into the darkness.

The first letters of each line in the poem spell **SPACE**.
Try to write your own poem in the same way.
Call it **P**
         L
         A
         N
         E
         T

97

Following instructions

Making a Möbius Strip

You need — a strip of paper about 25 cm by 3 cm
a paper clip
a pencil

1. Shade one side of the strip of paper.

2. Take the strip in your hands — one hand at each end.

3. Turn one end over, so that there is a half twist in the strip like this:

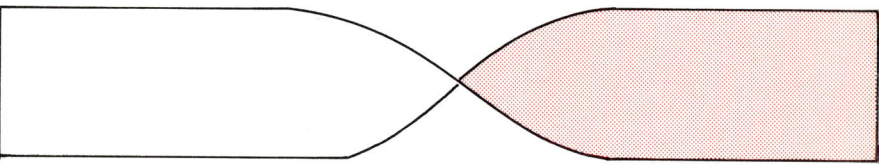

4. Bring the two ends to meet, shaded side to plain side.

5. Clip them together.

6. Draw a continuous line along the strip, without taking the pencil off the paper.

What do you find?

Talk about these instructions.
How would you change them to make them clearer?

98

The company words keep

Adam's class was asked to think of as many words as possible which might be used if writing or talking about the *idea* of **happiness**.
Here are some of the answers they gave:

joy	**birthday**	**happy**
Christmas	**bright**	**glowing**
jolly	**sailing**	**laughter**

Can you see why these words have something to do with **happiness**?

Talk about the words. How many more can you think of which fit the idea of **happiness**?

Next, Adam's class was asked to suggest *ideas* which they thought were **happy**.
Here are some of the ideas they thought of.
Adam: My Mum coming home from hospital.
Joyce: Children's faces on Christmas morning.
Annie: An old couple sitting by the fire with their cat.
Lewis: Throwing sticks for my dog on a summer day.

Can you see why these ideas are **happy** ones?

With your friends, talk about the words which you might use if you were talking or writing about the *idea* of **excitement**.
How many can you think of?

What *ideas* can you think of which are **exciting** ideas?

The way words are built

The English language has many words in it which are only used in certain places. Below are some of these words with their meanings, and the place where you might expect to hear them used.

fell	hill (northern England)
level	flat land (East Anglia)
dyke	wall (Scotland)
beck	stream (northern England)
fawcett	tap on a basin (USA)
beaut	good (Australia)
codding	pretending (Ireland)
dyke	ditch (northern England)
tup	male sheep (northern England)
clough	valley (northern England)
butty	sandwich (Lancashire)
bushranger	bandit (Australia)
byre	cowshed (New Zealand and Scotland)
pavement	roadway (Canada)

What word do *you* use for each of these?
Are there any members of your class who have come to your school from another part of the country or another country altogether?
Do they think any of the words you use are strange?

Children in New Zealand call the open sided shed in their school grounds a **shelter shed**.
What would it be called in your part of the world? Do you know of any other name for it?

The shoes we wear in the gym have many different names. In some parts of England they are called **plimsolls**, in other places **daps** or **pumps**. In some parts of Scotland they are called **gutties**. What do *you* call them?
Do you know any other name for them?

100

Mrs Frisby is a fieldmouse, a widow who lives with her young family in a hollow building block. Mrs Frisby's son Timothy is ill, and she has gone to see her husband's friend Mr Ages to get medicine. It is nearly evening and she has to get home. It is quite a long walk, and there are many dangers, including Dragon, the farmer's cat.

The story is taken from the book *Mrs Frisby and the Rats of NIMH*, by Robert C. O'Brien.

The crow and the cat

Mrs Frisby looked again at the sun and saw that she faced an unpleasant choice. She could go home by the same roundabout way she had come, in which case she would surely end up walking alone in the woods in the dark — a frightening prospect, for at night the forest was alive with danger. Then the owl came out to hunt, and foxes, weasels and strange wild cats stalked among the tree trunks.

The other choice would be dangerous, too, but with luck it would get her home before dark. That would be to take a straighter route, across the farmyard between the barn and the chicken house, going not too close to the house but cutting the distance by half. The cat would be there somewhere, but by daylight — and by staying in the open, away from the shrubs — she could probably spot him before he saw her.

The cat: He was called Dragon. Farmer Fitzgibbon's wife had given him the name as a joke when he was a small kitten pretending to be fierce. But when he grew up, the name turned out to be an apt one. He was enormous, with a huge, broad head and a large mouth full of curving fangs, needle sharp. He had seven claws on each foot and a thick, furry tail, which lashed angrily from side to side. In colour he was orange and white, with glaring yellow eyes; and when he leaped to kill, he gave a high, strangled scream that froze his victims where they stood.

But Mrs Frisby preferred not to think about that. Instead, as she came out of the woods from Mr Ages' house and reached the farmyard fence she thought about Timothy. She thought of how

his eyes shone with merriment when he made up small jokes, which he did frequently, and how invariably kind he was to his small, scatterbrained sister Cynthia. The other children sometimes laughed at her when she made mistakes, or grew impatient with her because she was forever losing things, but Timothy never did. Instead, he would help her find them. And when Cynthia herself had been sick in bed with a cold, he had sat by her side for hours and entertained her with stories. He made these up out of his head, and he seemed to have a bottomless supply of them.

Taking a firm grip on her packets of medicine, Mrs Frisby went under the fence and set out towards the farmyard. The first stretch was a long pasture; the barn itself, square and red and big, rose in the distance to her right; to her left, farther off were the chicken houses.

When at length she came abreast of the barn, she saw the wire fence that marked the other end of the pasture; and as she approached it, she was startled by a sudden outburst of noise. She thought at first it was a hen, strayed from the chickenyard — caught by a fox? She looked down the fence and saw that it was no hen at all, but a young crow, flapping in the grass, acting most oddly. As she watched, he fluttered to the top wire of the fence, where he perched nervously for a moment. Then he spread his wings, flapped hard, and took off — but after flying four feet he stopped with a snap and crashed to the ground again, shedding a flurry of black feathers and squawking loudly.

He was tied to the fence. A piece of something silvery — it looked like wire — was tangled around one of his legs; the other end of it was caught in the fence. Mrs Frisby walked closer, and then she could see it was not wire after all, but a length of silver-coloured string, probably left over from a Christmas package.

The crow was sitting on the fence, pecking ineffectively at the string with his bill, cawing softly to himself, a miserable sound. After a moment he spread his wings, and she could see he was going to try to fly again.

'Wait,' said Mrs Frisby.

The crow looked down and saw her in the grass.

'Why should I wait? Can't you see I'm caught? I've got to get loose.'

'But if you make so much noise again the cat is sure to hear. If he hasn't heard already.'

'You'd make a noise, too, if you were tied to a fence with a piece of string, and with night coming on.'

'I would not,' said Mrs Frisby, 'if I had any sense and knew there was a cat near by. Who tied you?' She was trying to calm the crow, who was obviously terrified.

He looked embarrassed and stared at his feet. 'I picked up the string. It got tangled with my foot. I sat on the fence to try to get it off, and it caught on the fence.'

'*Why* did you pick up the string?'

The crow, who was very young indeed — in fact, only a year old — said wearily. 'Because it was shiny.'

106

'You knew better.'

'I had been told.'

Birdbrain, thought Mrs Frisby, and then recalled what her husband used to say: The size of the brain is no measure of its capacity. And well she might recall it, for the crow's head was double the size of her own.

'Sit quietly,' she said. 'Look towards the house and see if you see the cat.'

'I don't see him. But I can't see behind the bushes. Oh, if I could just fly higher ...'

'Don't,' said Mrs Frisby. She looked at the sun; it was setting behind the trees. She thought of Timothy, and of the medicine.

she was carrying. Yet she knew she could not leave the foolish crow there to be killed — and killed he surely would be before sunrise — just for want of a few minutes' work. She might still make it by dusk if she hurried.

'Come down here,' she said. 'I'll get the string off.'

'How?' said the crow dubiously.

'Don't argue. I have only a few minutes.' She said this in a voice so authoritative that the crow fluttered down immediately.

'But if the cat comes ...' he said.

'If the cat comes, he'll knock you off the fence with one jump and catch you with the next. Be still.' She was already at work with her sharp teeth, gnawing at the string. It was twined and twisted and twined again around his right ankle, and she saw she would have to cut through it three times to get it off.

As she finished the second strand, the crow, who was staring towards the house, suddenly cried out:

'I see the cat!'

'*Quiet!*' whispered Mrs Frisby. 'Does he see us?'

'I don't know. Yes. He's looking at me. I don't think he can see you.'

'Stand perfectly still. Don't get in a panic.' She did not look up but started on the third strand.

'He's moving this way.'

'Fast or slow?'

'Medium. I think he's trying to figure out what I'm doing.'

She cut through the last strand, gave a tug, and the string fell off.

'There, you're free. Fly off, and be quick.'

'But what about you?'

'Maybe he hasn't seen me.'

'But he will. He's coming closer.'

Mrs Frisby looked around. There was not a bit of cover anywhere near, not a rock nor a hole nor a log; nothing at all

closer than the chicken yard — and that was in the direction the cat was coming from, and a long way off.

'Look,' said the crow. 'Climb on my back. Quick. And hang on.'

Mrs Frisby did what she was told, first grasping the precious packages of medicine tightly between her teeth.

'Are you on?'

'Yes.'

She gripped the feathers on his back, felt the beat of his powerful black wings, felt a dizzying upward surge, and shut her eyes tight.

'Just in time,' said the crow, and she heard the angry scream of the cat as he leaped at where they had just been. 'It's lucky you're so light. I can scarcely tell you're there.' Lucky indeed, thought Mrs Frisby; if it had not been for your foolishness I'd never have got into such a scrape. However, she thought it wise not to say so, under the circumstances.

'Where do you live?' asked the crow.

'In the garden patch. Near the big stone.'

'I'll drop you off there.' He banked alarmingly, and for a moment Mrs Frisby thought he meant it literally. But a few seconds later — so fast does the crow fly — they were gliding to earth a yard from her front door.

'Thank you very much,' said Mrs Frisby, hopping to the ground.

'It's I who should be thanking you,' said the crow. 'You saved my life.'

'And you mine.'

'Ah, but that's not quite even. Yours wouldn't have been risked if it had not been for me — and my piece of string.' And since this was just what she had been thinking, Mrs Frisby did not argue.

'We all help one another against the cat,' she said.

'True. Just the same, I am in debt to you. If the time ever comes when I can help you, I hope you will ask me. My name is Jeremy. Mention it to any crow you see in these woods and he will find me.'

'Thank you,' said Mrs Frisby, 'I will remember.'

Jeremy flew away to the woods, and she entered her house, taking the three doses of medicine with her.

To think and talk about

A 1. Read the part of the story again which tells about the cat. How suitable is the name Dragon? In what ways is Dragon different from other cats?

2. In what ways is Timothy different from Mrs Frisby's other children?
    What does this tell us about Timothy?

3. In her dealings with the crow, Mrs Frisby is very calm. The crow is quite the opposite. How many reasons can you find for Mrs Frisby's calmness in the face of danger?

4. What does Mrs Frisby think of the crow? How many clues can you find which tell you?

5. What dangers face Mrs Frisby in her life? In what ways does she try to avoid them?

6. Jeremy the crow says at the end that it was his fault that Mrs Frisby's life had been risked. Is this really true?

B 1. Would you have helped the crow, if you had been Mrs Frisby? Can you see reasons why she should not help?

2. Imagine you are Jeremy. How would you have felt when caught by the piece of string? How would you have felt about Mrs Frisby?

3. 'We all help one another against the cat.' Does this mean any more than it says? Why does Mrs Frisby say it?

4. In what ways could Jeremy's friendship be helpful to Mrs Frisby in the future?

5. Did you enjoy the story, 'The Crow and the Cat'? What did you like about it? What did you not like?

More books to read

1. *The Snow House* by N. Wilkinson
   There's a mouse circus in this story. All but one of a family of mice are captured by the man who runs this circus.

2. *Manxmouse* by Paul Gallico
   The story of the adventures of a china mouse who comes to life!

3. *Children of Green Knowe* by Lucy M. Boston
   Tolly was to spend Christmas with his great-grandmother in what looked like a lonely place. Read how it turned out not to be lonely because of a special kind of magic.

Making words

How many new words can you make, using only letters found in

FLAGPOLE?

To write about

Imagine that one day you see a mouse under the table. You get down to look at it, but when you do, to your amazement it turns round, fixes you with icy eye, and says, 'Did your mother not teach you that it is *very rude* to stare?'
Write the story of the talking mouse.

How on earth!

Talk about the strange scene in this picture.
How did it happen?
Could you write a story about it?

Apostrophes

Can you put the apostrophe in the right place in each of these sentences?

1. Dads car is broken down.

2. We wouldnt want to play with you anyway!

3. Dont ever try to cross the road without looking for traffic.

4. Lauras lip trembled as she faced her father.

5. Joes new shoes were pinching his feet terribly.

Anne and the field-mouse

We found a mouse in the chalk quarry today
In a circle of stones and empty oil drums
By the fag ends of a fire. There had been
A picnic there; he must have been after the crumbs.

Jane saw him first, a flicker of brown fur
In and out of the charred wood and chalk-white.
I saw him last, but not till we'd turned up
Every stone and surprised him into flight,

Though not far — little zigzag spurts from stone
To stone. Once, as he lurked in his hiding-place,
I saw his beady eyes uplifted to mine.
I'd never seen such terror in so small a face.

I watched, amazed and guilty. Beside us suddenly
A heavy pheasant whirred up from the ground,
Scaring us all; and, before we knew it, the mouse
Had broken cover, skimming away without a sound,

Melting into the nettles. We didn't go
Till I'd chalked in capitals on a rusty can:
THERE'S A MOUSE IN THOSE NETTLES. LEAVE
HIM ALONE. NOVEMBER 15TH. ANNE.

Ian Serraillier

Searching for missing words

In the passage some words have been missed out.
Can you be sure which words have been missed out?
Sometimes there can be only one answer.
Sometimes there can be several answers for you to think and talk about.
How many words can you find?

Timothy's gaze was fixed on the sky. Eagerly he scanned the vast expanse of grey. If Tiptoes _____ he would brave his mother's disapproval and _____ him home again. When she heard the _____ surely she would let him stay a _____longer. But no wheeling pigeon came into _____. The only airborne creatures were a flight_____ starlings making for their nightly roosting _____ and a huddle of sparrows noisily enjoying a _____ in the shallow reaches of the pond. _____ heart sank. Without saying goodbye to the _____ keeper and with the empty wicker basket _____ from his hand he turned towards the _____ iron park gates. Tiptoes had vanished for _____.

From *Timothy and Tiptoes* by Irene Byers

Word pairs

Below are two sets of words. Each word in set A has a partner in set B which sounds exactly the same, although it is spelt differently. Can you write down the partners?

Set A	Set B
stair	red
scene	herd
fore	four
heard	muscle
read	stare
mussel	seen

Fact or opinion?

When you are reading, it is important to know the difference between fact and opinion. Often what someone *thinks* or *feels* about something can be written as if it were *true*. Here are some more sentences some of which are **facts** and some **opinions**. Sort them into two groups
   (a) Facts
   (b) Opinions

1. The 1980 Olympic Games were held in Moscow.

2. The Americans were represented by their best ever team.

3. The most beautiful city in Europe is Venice.

4. The tallest building in the world is in America.

5. No city should be bigger than London is already.

6. The fact that many people refuse to work hard is cause for great worry.

7. Britain and Europe should be linked by a tunnel.

8. Much of Australia is desert land.

Cynddylan on a tractor

Ah, you should see Cynddylan on a tractor.
Gone the old look that yoked him to the soil;
He's a new man now, part of the machine,
His nerves metal and his blood oil.
The clutch curses, but the gears obey
His least bidding, and lo, he's away
Out of the farmyard, scattering hens.
Riding to work now as a great man should,
He is the knight at arms breaking the fields'
Mirror of silence, emptying the wood
Of foxes and squirrels and bright jays.
The sun comes over the tall trees
Kindling all the hedges, but not for him
Who runs his engine on a different fuel.
And all the birds are singing, bills wide in vain,
As Cynddylan passes proudly up the lane.

R. S. Thomas

Sort it out

Here are two groups of sentences which make a story.
They are in the wrong order.
Can you write the stories in the correct order?

1. (a) Then they all saw that the ants were everywhere. Leon
        quickly started to gather up the food.

    (b) Paul felt something nipping his ankles.

    (c) She was the first to notice the unwelcome army which
        was marching over the cloth.

    (d) The spread of cakes and sandwiches was magnificent.

    (e) Excitedly the children sat round the cloth which was
        placed on the ground.

    (f) Just as she started to munch a ham roll Jean screamed.

    (g) The others retreated to the road, cross that their picnic
        had been ruined by these tiny creatures.

2. (a) Later in the morning, if the weather was fair, he would sit
        on the quayside reading.

    (b) Each day at about the same time the old sea captain
        marched along the promenade.

    (c) The small newsagent's was his first call and he emerged
        from there with his newspaper under his arm.

    (d) He gazed out to sea as he made his way and frequently
        breathed deeply throwing his shoulders back at the
        same time.

    (e) He would frequently buy a pint of milk before making the
        return journey to his small cottage.

    (f) Often he would pause in his reading to search the skyline
        and remember his great days at sea.

Points of view

Tea-time Treat

Kathy and Peter decide to play a trick on their mother. They mix some soap powder into the flour in the kitchen. That afternoon their mother announces that she has baked them their favourite cake as a surprise and that they can invite some of their friends to tea. Kathy and Peter daren't explain what they have done, but their mother wonders why they look so miserable. Tea starts and their friend Sue takes the first bite from the cake.

What happens then? Imagine you are
    (a) Kathy or Peter
or (b) mother
or (c) Sue

Give or write an account of the incident from your point of view.

Crossword

Can you make up clues for this crossword?

Across

1.

4.

5.

7.

Down

1.

2.

3.

6.

¹g	u	²a	r	³d
u	■	n	■	a
⁴e	l	k	■	r
s	■	⁵l	⁶i	e
⁷t	r	e	s	s

Ideas to write about

1. Imagine you are Jeremy.
   How did the story start for you?
   How do you feel about Mrs Frisby?
   Write the story from Jeremy's point of view.

2. It is very dangerous for Mrs Frisby to be out in the woods at night.
   Write another adventure of Mrs Frisby in which she is in the woods at night.
   How does she escape this time?

3. This picture is part of a story.
   Talk about the story which the picture might come into.
   Who are the children?
   How do they come to be on a magic carpet?
   Where are they going? Why?
   Write the story.

Reading for the main idea

Philip was working on a project about **giraffes** and came across this passage in a book.

The giraffe is the tallest of all animals, its long neck helping it to eat leaves from the tops of trees. Nibbling grass or drinking from a stream is not so straightforward, however. First this unusual creature has to spread its long front legs apart in order to lower its head to ground level. The beautiful body markings act as an excellent means of camouflage. When standing still among the trees the patches of sunlight and shadow blend so efficiently with the patterns on its skin that it becomes almost invisible. Another helpful feature is the eyes, which stick out quite far from both sides of its skull, helping this shy animal to see behind it without having to turn its head.

Philip made notes of the main ideas in the story. Here is what he wrote:
— **tallest of animals**
— **giraffe**
— **long neck useful.**

Think of the other main ideas in the story. Add them to Philip's list so that you have notes of all the main ideas.
Can you use your notes to write your own shortened version of the passage — 'The Giraffe'?

Act it out

Imagine Mrs Frisby is telling her family the story of her journey.
Can you say what the important parts of the story are?
How do you think she would tell it to her family?
Do you think she would leave anything out?

What will the young mice think of the story?
Perhaps they will be surprised at some of what they hear.
What questions will they ask?
Perhaps they will be frightened by some of what they hear.
How will they show their fright?

With some friends, could you try acting the scene when Mrs
Frisby tells the tale of her adventure?

Here is a poem by a girl called Sophie.

In the woods

Children's laughter came from
The far side
But where I sat was silent
with silent sounds

The silent scurry of silent feet
The silent sighing of the breeze
The silent bird song
Soothed me to silent sleep

On that summer day
In the woods.

Why not try writing a poem of your own about a memory of
summer?

The company words keep

Jill was interested in certain ideas in the story 'The Crow and the Cat'. They were:

fear   **flying**   **woods**

Jill wanted to find as many words as she could which were connected with these ideas.
Here is how she started:

fear	flying	woods
shiver	soar	dark
chill	high	menacing
fright	take off	gloomy
run	crash	dank

Can you add to Jill's lists?

The way words are built

There are many interesting place names.
Some are pronounced in a very different way from that in which
they are spelt. Below are some examples. A rough guide to
pronunciation is given in brackets.

Beauvoir	(Beever)
Llanelli	(Klanethlee)
Alnwick	(Anik)
Milngavie	(Milguy)
Brough	(Bruff)
Beaulieu	(Bewlee)
Keighley	(Keethlee)
Worcester	(Wooster)
Ahoghill	(Achawhill)
Mousehole	(Mowsell)

There are many towns or villages with names which, like those
above, are spelt differently from the way they are said. Try to
find examples of this near where you live. A map of your area
may help you.

Discuss how the names are said and spelt. Can anyone suggest a
reason why this happens?

Acknowledgements

Prose

pp.   2–8   *Farmer Giles of Ham,* J. R. R.Tolkein, Allen and Unwin
pp. 28–34   *How the Whale Became,* Ted Hughes, Faber and Faber
pp. 50–58   *James and the Giant Peach,* Roald Dahl, Allen and Unwin/Penguin
pp. 78–84   *Rebecca's World,* Terry Nation, G. Whizzard Publications
pp. 102–10   *Mrs Frisby and the Rats of NIMH,* Robert C. O'Brien, Gollancz

Poetry

p. 12   'Giant Thunder' by James Reeves, *The Blackbird in the Lilac,* OUP
p. 17   'My dad's thumb' by Michael Rosen, *Mind Your Own Business,* Deutsch
pp. 38–9   'In the bee factory' by Libby Houston, *Stories and Rhymes,* BBC
p. 45   'The game of life' by Roy Fuller, *Poor Roy,* Deutsch
p. 61   'The ladybird' by Clive Sansom, *The Golden Unicorn,* Methuen
pp. 70–71 'Earthworm' by Leonard Clark, *Collected Poems and Verses,* Dobson
p. 96   'The Marrog' by R. C. Scriven, *Stories and Rhymes,* BBC
p. 114   'Anne and the fieldmouse' by Ian Serraillier, *Happily Ever After,* OUP
p. 117   'Cynddlyan on a tractor' by R. S. Thomas, *Song at the Year's Turning,*
           Granada

Pictures

pp. 21, 53, 56, 57, 81, 84   Illustrations by David Farris
p. 92   'Hunters in the snow' by Pieter Breugel, reproduced by permission of the
            Kunsthistorisches Museum, Vienna